U.S. Fish & Wildlife Service

A Preliminary Biological Assessment of Kirwin National Wildlife Refuge

Biological Technical Publication

BTP-R6004-2004

Murray K. Laubhan

U.S. Geological Survey, Northern Prairie Wildlife Research Center

8711 37th Street SE, Jamestown, North Dakota, USA 58401

Author Contact information:
Murray K. Laubhan, U.S. Geological Survey,
Northern Prairie Wildlife Research Center, 8711 37th
St. SE, Jamestown, ND 58401.
Phone: 701/ 253 5534,
Fax: 701/ 253 5553
Email: murray_laubhan@usgs.gov.

For additional copies or information, contact:
Wayne J. King, USFWS Region 6, Regional Refuge
Biologist. P.O. Box 25486 Denver Federal Center
Denver, Colorado 80225-0486
Phone: 303/236 8102
Fax: 303/236 4792
Email: wayne_j_king@fws.gov

Recommended citation:
Laubhan, M. K. 2004. A preliminary biological
assessment of Kirwin National Wildlife Refuge,
Phillipsburg, Kansas. U.S. Department of Interior,
Fish and Wildlife Service, Biological Technical
Publication, BTP-R6004-2004, Washington, D.C.

Series Senior Technical Editor:
Stephanie L. Jones, USFWS, Region 6 , Nongame
Migratory Bird Coordinator, P.O. Box 25486 Denver
Federal Center Denver, Colorado 80225-0486

Associate Editor:
Wayne J. King, Regional Refuge Biologist USFWS,
Region 6, P.O. Box 25486, Denver Federal Center,
Denver, Colorado 80225-0486

Table of Contents

Summary

This report represents an initial biological assessment of Kirwin National Wildlife Refuge (NWR) conducted as part of the pre-planning phase for development of a Comprehensive Conservation Plan (CCP). Stimulation for the report was based on the concept that future decisions related to the biological portion of the CCP will be based on the best available science. Therefore, an attempt is made to integrate information from many different scientific disciplines (e.g., geology, hydrology, biology) to help identify ecological constraints and opportunities imposed by the land base being considered. Consequently, there is a greater likelihood of identifying potential shortcomings of various management actions during the decision making process.

Information in this report is based on a relatively limited number of published articles, past notes, and observations. An attempt was made to locate sufficient relevant information necessary to formulate more definitive ideas and provide additional context. Thus, the information provided below is known to be incomplete and a more thorough synthesis will be required. Further, interpretation of published information can vary among individuals and the refuge staff is encouraged to review the documents cited in this report. Their years of observation and experience managing the refuge are invaluable to ensuring that information used to make decisions is applicable. Consequently, some sections contain information that was not fully explored in the evaluation section; however, it was retained because it may be useful as the refuge staff and core CCP team examines different management options. Finally, decisions regarding management of each individual community should be combined and evaluated collectively to identify potential conflicts. Although this may seem simple and straightforward, this task often is difficult because it frequently requires an iterative approach to ensure that important issues have not been omitted.

This report does not contain conclusions, nor does it advocate any opinions (favorable or unfavorable) regarding the biological program. Further, concepts such as alternatives, goals, and objectives, are not discussed. The core CCP team will address these topics. Rather, it represents a summary that hopefully will be used to focus future discussion regarding biological data needs and approaches for using this information to make decisions. Ultimately, however, scientific information alone will not lead to a definitive decision regarding future direction, because biology is only one of many components that must be considered in the evaluation. Therefore, it is recommended that U. S. Fish and Wildlife Service (FWS) personnel responsible for determining the future direction of the refuge be consulted to establish guidelines and agree on the approach that will be used in evaluating the biological program prior to proceeding.

Acknowledgments

Prior to writing the report, the author was invited to the refuge for a two-day meeting with Erich Gilbert (refuge manager), Craig Mowry (assistant refuge manager), and Wayne King (regional refuge biologist). The purpose was to become familiar with the site, discuss management opportunities and constraints, and identify potential types of information that would assist the staff in developing a credible biological plan to guide future management. These individuals contributed significant time and insight regarding management of the refuge. The assistance of Rachel Lambhan and Mark Fly in locating and processing information used in this report is greatly appreciated. Thanks also to the following individuals for providing reviews of an earlier draft: E. Gilbert, R. A. Gleason, S. L. Jones, W. J. King, R.A. Laubhan, C. Mowry, D. M. Mushet, and J. D. Petty.

Introduction

Stimulation for this report was generated by passage of the 1997 National Wildlife Refuge System Improvement Act (NWRSIA) that requires each refuge in the National Wildlife Refuge System to develop a CCP that includes goals and objectives that are based on the best available science. To accomplish this mandate, Region 6 of FWS contracted with the Biological Resources Division of the U. S. Geological Survey (USGS) to inspect refuge habitats and synthesize available information pertinent to the management of Kirwin NWR as part of a pre-planning phase to guide development of a CCP. This report represents such a synthesis.

The brevity of the site visit did not allow for detailed discussions between USGS and FWS personnel, but it did provide the opportunity to exchange thoughts regarding the information needed to evaluate the biological program. Thus, the ideas contained within this report are of a general nature and should be viewed as a collaborative effort that involved the refuge staff. Additional work will be required to objectively evaluate the biological program, and this report should be viewed as an initial effort to start this process. In addition, there are alternative ways of approaching an evaluation that would require different levels and types of information. Therefore, the responsibility of FWS is to review the report and other relevant materials, discuss available options with appropriate personnel, and determine if the identified information needs and recommendations outlined in this report are acceptable and represent the preferred manner of proceeding.

General descriptive information on refuge establishment, topography, climate, geology, soils, vegetation, and wildlife is intended to provide a brief background of the refuge with regard to functions, processes, and values. This information is important as a baseline for understanding the impact of past land alterations and for developing management guidelines for the future. In contrast, the section on conservation is intended to provide perspective regarding potential refuge contributions to natural resources based on conservation plans that have been developed for application at larger geographic scales that encompass the refuge. The section on evaluation of community types discusses in more detail the attributes of various communities that occur within the refuge boundary. For ease of discussion, four broad communities were delineated as follows: (1) Reservoir Pool, (2) Shoreline, (3) Riparian, and (4) Upland. For each community, a brief synopsis of historic and current conditions is provided. Also, potential management options are discussed along with some associated benefits and detriments. Appendix A summarizes the information needs that may be required to address the recommendations provided in the evaluation section. These recommendations largely are those of the author and are based on thoughts that resulted from discussions with FWS personnel during the site visit trip in March. Therefore, the list is incomplete from a biological perspective and largely ignores recreational and other considerations. Additional effort will be required by FWS personnel to identify and integrate issues, concerns, and recommendations through internal discussions and public scoping. Although some scoping has already occurred, hopefully this report will assist future efforts by providing some background biological information. Obviously, this represents only the first step in a long process and additional work is necessary.

Description

Refuge Establishment and Authorities

Kirwin NWR is an overlay project on a U. S. Bureau of Reclamation (BOR) irrigation and flood control reservoir known as Kirwin (U. S. Fish and Wildlife Service, URL http://kirwin.fws.gov/refugemap.htm). The reservoir was constructed before irrigation became widely practiced (Christensen 1999). Dedicated in 1955, the reservoir has a contributing drainage area of 3,540 km² (1,367 mi²) and a total water storage capacity of 38,797 ha-m (314,550 ac-ft). The storage capacity is allocated among flood control (36.532 ha-m [215,115 ac-ft]), conservation storage (11,057 ha-m [89,650 ac-ft]), and inactive or dead storage (1,207 ha-m [9,785 ac-ft]) (Christensen 1999). Kirwin NWR was established in 1954 pursuant to the Fish and Wildlife Coordination Act (16 U.S.C. ¤ 664) for the "…conservation, maintenance, and management of wildlife, resources thereof, and its habitat thereon,…" (U. S. Fish and Wildlife Service, URL http://refuges.fws.gov/policymakers/). The BOR owns the land and controls reservoir water levels, whereas the refuge staff manages all other activities on the land and water (U. S. Bureau of Reclamation, URL http://www.usbr.gov/gp).

Location and Topography

The 4,366-ha (10,788 ac) refuge includes Kirwin Reservoir and bordering areas in southeast Phillips County, Kansas. Topography of the area is characterized by rolling hills, the gently sloping Kirwin terrace, and a narrow river valley formed by the North Fork of the Solomon River (Leonard 1952, Christensen 1999). The refuge encompasses portions of the North Fork Solomon River and Bow Creek. These rivers drain an area of 359,874 ha (889,248 ac) above the reservoir (U.S. Bureau of Reclamation 2002). The altitude of the terrace ranges from an elevation of 602 m (1,975 ft) in Phillips County to 445 m (1,460 ft) in Mitchell County. The gradient of the North Fork Solomon River channel is about 1.3 m/km (7.1 ft/mi) in Phillips County.

The refuge is located in the North Fork Solomon River Sub-Basin. The North Fork Solomon originates in western Thomas County, Kansas, approximately 193 km (120 mi) west of Kirwin Dam and drains an area of 3,556 km² (1,373 mi²) (U.S. Bureau of Reclamation 2002). Elevation of the area ranges from about 430 m (1,410 ft) at the mouth of North Fork Solomon River in Mitchell County, to about 640 m (2,100 ft) in the western part of Phillips County. Like other valleys in north-central Kansas, the North Fork Solomon valley and its tributaries are asymmetrical and typically have precipitous south walls and gently sloping north walls. According to Leonard (1952) the valley consists of broad undissected terraces and a floodplain width that varies from 201-805 m (660-2,640 ft). The relief from the stream channel to the top of the Kirwin terrace, which lies above flood level, is as much as 12 m (40 ft). The Kirwin terrace slopes gently (gradient = 1.4 m/km [7.3 ft/mile]), is

moderately well drained, and represents the primary area of cultivated farmland. Historically, the elevation of the floodplain varied between 4.6-7.6 m (15-25 ft) below the Kirwin terrace and 3.7-4.9 m (12-16 ft) above the water level of the river. Many of the ephemeral streams that drain the uplands disappear on the surface of the terrace, which suggests these streams contribute a large part of their water to the groundwater reservoir in the area.

Agriculture and ranching have been the primary economic forces in the area since the early 1800's (U.S. Bureau of Reclamation 2002). In Phillips County, the land in farms (220,398 ha [554,603 ac]) accounted for 97.8% of the county land base (229,478 ha [567,040 ac]) in 1997. Further, of the land in farms, cropland (130,329 ha [322,043 ac]) accounted for 56.8% of the county land base (U. S. Bureau of Reclamation 2002). Representative crops produced in Phillips County during 1997 included corn, sorghum, wheat, oats, soybeans, and hay (U. S. Department of Agriculture National Agricultural Statistics Services, URL http://www.nass.usda.gov/census/census97/highlights/ks/ksc074.txt).

The drainage area below the reservoir is 348,004 ha (859,918 ac), of which 6,325 ha (1.8%; 15,630 ac) is irrigated (Christensen 1999). The BOR operates Kirwin Irrigation District Number 1 downstream from the reservoir and provides surface water outflow to irrigate as much as 4,650 ha (11,490 ac) of farmland (U.S. Bureau of Reclamation 2002) that generally is within 8 km (5 mi) of the North Fork Solomon River (Christensen 1999). As mentioned previously, the drainage area above the reservoir is 359,874 ha (889,248 ac), of which 24,525 ha (6.8%; 60,600 ac) is irrigated. The use of surface water for irrigation first occurred in 1928 with the establishment of two pumping plants, but by 1946 a total 13 plants had been established (Leonard 1952). Currently, the primary source of irrigation water is from alluvial wells, which have increased from <10 in 1949 to >150 in 1993 (U.S. Bureau of Reclamation 2002).

The North Fork Solomon Sub-Basin is part of the Solomon River Basin, which extends across parts of 17 Kansas counties and includes the Solomon River and its major tributaries, the North Fork and South Fork Solomon Rivers. The rivers and associated tributaries drain approximately 17,716 km² (6,840 mi²) of mainly agricultural land (Christensen 1999). In addition to Kirwin Reservoir, the BOR also operates two additional reservoirs in the basin; Webster Reservoir on the South Fork Solomon River and Waconda Lake at the confluence of the North and South Fork Solomon Rivers. The three reservoirs provide water for irrigation, municipal, industrial, and domestic use; flood control; recreation; and fish and wildlife habitat (Christensen 1999).

The elevation of the basin varies from approximately 1,006 m (3,300 ft) in the west to 351 m (1,150 ft) in the east near the town of Solomon, Kansas. The average gradient of the region is approximately 2.7-2.8 m/km (14-15 ft/mi). The average gradient for the main stem

Solomon River is 0.9 m/km (5 ft/mi) (U.S. Bureau of Reclamation 2002). Both the North Fork and South Fork Solomon Rivers derive their flows from precipitation runoff and groundwater discharge from underlying aquifers (U.S. Bureau of Reclamation 2002).

Finally, the Solomon River Basin is located in both the Smoky Hills and High Plains Physiographic Regions of the Great Plains Physiographic Province (Launchbaugh and Owensby 1978). The High Plains region of Kansas extends from the western state line eastward into Graham County. The topography is characterized by flat to gently rolling hills with narrow, shallow valleys of low relief. Sand, gravel, and porous rock cover most of the region. The Smoky Hills Region, which encompasses Kirwin NWR, is composed of three distinct hill ranges. Steep chalk bluffs characterize the western range of hills, whereas Greenhorn Limestone and Dakota Sandstone cap the middle and eastern range of hills, respectively. The eastern boundary of the Smoky Hills Region is in Clay County and is adjacent to the Flint Hills Physiographic Region (Kansas Geological Survey, URL http://www.kgs.ukans.edu/Physio/physio.html). Vegetation communities within this region are classified as mixed-grass prairie with forested river bottoms (Kuchler 1974).

Climate
The climate of the Solomon Basin is classified as subhumid. Summers are characterized by hot days and cool evenings, whereas winters are normally moderate with light snowfall and only occasional short periods of severe cold. The average length of the growing season is about 167 days (Leonard 1952) and the frost-free period extends from 29 April to 13 October (Albertson 1937). Long-term climate data (5/1/1952 – 12/31/2002) was obtained from the National Climate Data Center cooperative station located at Kirwin Dam (http://lwf.ncdc.noaa.gov/oa/climate/, station # 144357). The mean monthly maximum temperature ranged from 3.1 C(37.5°F) in January to 33.4°C (92.2°F) in July, whereas mean monthly minimum temperature ranged from -11.3°C (11.6°F) in January to 17.8 °C (64.0°F) in July.

Average annual precipitation during this period was 58.5 cm (23.0 in), with 44.2% of total annual precipitation occurring in May (mean = 10.2 cm [4.0 in]), June (mean = 7.8 cm [3.1 in]), and July (mean = 7.7 cm [3.0 in]). However, not all of this moisture is necessarily available for plant growth because evaporation is also occurring during these months. Graphs obtained from the National Oceanic and Atmospheric Administration (URL http://www.noaa.gov), which depict ranges of evaporation for the entire U.S, were used to obtain a coarse estimate of 28.2 cm (11.1 in) of annual evaporation for north-central Kansas. Months with highest evaporative losses were June (5.6 cm [2.2 in]), July (6.1 cm [2.4 in]), and August (5.6 cm [2.2 in]).

The Palmer Drought Severity Index (PDSI) was developed to represent the severity of dry and wet periods based on monthly temperature and precipitation data as well as the water holding capacity of soils at a location (Palmer 1965). Thus, this measure provides a method integrating the above information. For north-central Kansas, the long-term PDSI (1895-2002) indicates cyclic patterns of drought and wetness. During 1989 and 1990, portions of 1991, and for a brief period in 2001, this region experienced severe drought, but from late 1993 through mid-1994 the area was extremely wet (National Climate Data Center, URL http://lwf.ncdc.noaa.gov/oa/climate/).

Geology
The surface geology of the Solomon Basin consists of unconsolidated and consolidated rocks. The unconsolidated surface deposits consist of Quaternary alluvium, loess, and the Tertiary Ogallala Formation, whereas Cretaceous and Permian rocks form the bedrock. In general, the basin is underlain by strata of marine origin (Christensen 1999). The dendritic and asymmetrical drainage pattern of the Solomon River suggests the lack of faults and folds and the presence of flat underlying rock units (U.S. Bureau of Reclamation 1984).

The Greenhorn Limestone, Graneros Shale, and Dakota Sandstone outcrop as far east as western Clay County, Kansas. Permian beds outcrop in counties farther east. The Greenhorn Limestone consists of alternating beds of calcareous shale and chalky limestone. The Graneros Shale is noncalcareous, fissile shale with sandstone lenses. The Dakota Formation consists of lenticular sandstone bodies that are embedded in mudstone. Generally, the sandstones are fine to medium grained, well sorted, and exhibit cross-bedding (Kansas Department of Agriculture Division of Water Resources), URL http://www.accesskansas.org/kda/dwr/).

The North Fork Solomon River is underlain by, or incised into, Cretaceous beds that generally dip to the west, whereas the erosional surface generally slopes to the east. The oldest subsurface rocks at the eastern end of the basin are of the Sumner Group. Above the Sumner Group is Cretaceous marine sediment beginning with the Dakota Formation, which is overlain by the Cheyenne Sandstone, Kiowa Shale, Graneros Shale, Greenhorn Limestone, and Carlile Shale. The Carlile Shale is exposed in stream valleys in Phillips County. Above the Carlile Shale is the Niobrara Formation, which is exposed in much of the North Fork Solomon River Basin (Leonard 1952), and the Pierre shale, of which there is only one known small outcrop in the basin upstream from Webster Reservoir (Moore and Landes 1937, Ross 1991). The Pierre Shale lies conformably on the Niobrara Chalk, which is a gray, shaly, fossiliferous chalk with weathered surfaces. The chalk contains bentonite beds and limonite concretions (Kansas Department of Agriculture Division of Water Resources).

The north and south divides of the Solomon River are capped by remnants of the Ogallala formation in the western part of the Solomon Basin, whereas the uplands and valley walls over much of north-central

Kansas are composed of loess of the Sanborn formation that was deposited during glacial retreat (Leonard 1952). The Ogallala formation was formed during the Pliocene by eastward flowing streams that filled pre-existing valleys with alluvial sediments. Continued deposition of alluvial sediments formed a broad alluvial plain. The Ogallala consists mainly of silt, sand, gravel, and "mortar beds" formed by cementation of sediments with calcium carbonate. However, lenticular beds of well-sorted sand, gravel, bentonite, and volcanic ash also exist. The Ogallala lies unconformably on the Pierre Shale in the western part of the basin and on the Niobrara Formation in the eastern part of the basin. The surface of the Ogallala dips to the east-northeast and the average gradient is 2.1 m/km (11 ft/mi) (Kansas Department of Agriculture Division of Water Resources).

Narrow belts of alluvium, most of Recent age, are adjacent to the Solomon River channel and its tributaries and occupy the floodplain (Leonard 1952). The alluvium consists mainly of gravel, sand, silt, and some clay. However, loess also may occur along major streams. The loess is underlain by stream-deposited sands that are in a high terrace position with respect to the valleys (Leonard 1952). At several places in the floodplain, wind has deposited sand from the alluvium into dunes or in thin layers that cover the terrace surfaces (Leonard 1952). These areas of sand deposition occur in Phillips County, but thickness of the fluvial and loess deposits is < 3.0 m (10 ft) (Kansas Department of Agriculture Division of Water Resources). A map illustrating the locations of these geologic features on the refuge was developed by Johnson and Arbogast (1993) and can be obtained from the Kansas Geological Survey (URL http://www.kgs.ukans.edu/General/Geology/County/nop/phillips.html).

Groundwater

The Sanborn formation, which consists of a thin layer of loess that overlies Cretaceous rocks, is a locally important source of groundwater (Leonard 1952). The most important aquifer in the area, however, occurs in the deposits underlying the Kirwin terrace surface. In general, this terrace is underlain by 9.1-27.4 m (30-90 ft) of unconsolidated deposits (e.g., coarse textured sand and gravel) that is quite permeable and lies below the water table (Leonard 1952). The broad, nearly flat terrace surface constitutes a large recharge area and streams that originate in nearby hills contribute additional recharge. Groundwater moves laterally through the terrace deposits and into the alluvium or into the channel of North Fork Solomon River. Thus, the water table in the Recent alluvium is continuous with the water table in the terrace deposits and with the water level in the flowing streams. The coarse nature of the alluvium makes it an important potential source of groundwater (Leonard 1952). Hydraulic conductivity has been estimated at 51.8 m/day (170 ft/day) with an average transmissivity of 241.5 m²/day (2,600 ft²/day) (Phillips 1980). Well yields vary from 38-1893 l/min (10-500 gal/min).

The water table in the valley slopes from east to west, and from the sides of the valley toward the center. The downstream slope of the water table varies from about 2.2 m/km (11.5 ft/mi) in western Phillips County to about 1.2 m/km (6.4 ft/mi) near the town of Kirwin (Leonard 1952). Most ephemeral streams in the area are above the water table and, when flowing, probably contribute some water to the groundwater. In contrast, the Solomon River and Bow Creek are gaining streams (e.g., flow in these streams is partially maintained by groundwater that seeps into the channel) (Leonard 1952).

Soils

In north-central Kansas, soils are composed primarily of Mollisols in the suborder Ustolls. A dark surface horizon rich in bases are primary characteristics of Mollisols. Nearly all have a mollic epipedon, but many also have an argillic, nitric, or calcic horizon. Specifically, soils of the North Solomon Valley are primarily fertile, silty clay loams derived from reworked loess (Leonard 1952), some of which are rich in selenium (U. S. Geological Survey, URL http://ks.water.usgs.gov/Kansas/studies/ressed/). The soils in valleys are slightly sloping, friable, and generally have high agricultural productivity. In the western and central parts of the basin, soils are generally friable and relatively impermeable, with some silt loam and loess. The more level soils in the western and central parts of the basin are used for grain cultivation and are moderately productive. The soils in the eastern part of the basin range from shallow sands to thick clays and generally have low agricultural productivity (U.S. Bureau of Reclamation 1984).

Vegetation

Historically, the floodplains of both rivers supported woody vegetation, tall grasses, and forbs, whereas the uplands largely were mixed-grass prairie (Kuchler 1974). However, human settlement and associated land use activities altered historic processes and, ultimately, the plant and wildlife communities. Although construction of the reservoir in 1952 represents an obvious perturbation that altered various ecological aspects of the rivers and associated floodplains, alteration of the uplands also occurred prior to refuge establishment. The area surrounding Kirwin NWR was cultivated extensively and also was used to pasture cattle prior to 1945 (Leonard 1952). The general location of these activities was related to topography and soils. Much of the cultivation occurred on the terrace due to the presence of fertile, moderately well drained soils. In contrast, cattle production typically occurred on areas bordering the valley where cultivation was prevented because of steep gradients or presence of rocky soil formed on chalk and limestone rocks (Leonard 1952). Although a detailed history of past land use was not developed for the refuge, a study conducted by Rezsutek (1990) supports this scenario. He reports that lands composing the refuge were formerly family farms and much of the native grassland in the area had been turned under for the production of crops prior to establishment. Further, although J. Launchbaugh (in

K. Launchbaugh's field notes) described some areas as "native prairie", Rezsutek (1990) suggests they may have been "restored prairie".

Grassland, cropland, deepwater and shoreline habitats of the reservoir, and riparian zones bordering the tributary rivers are dominant communities on the refuge. In addition, shelterbelts, palustrine wetlands, and chalk bluffs also occur within the refuge boundary. When the reservoir is at conservation pool (527.1 m [1729.25 ft]) there are 2,050 ha (5,065 ac) of surface water and about 60 km (37 mi) of shoreline. According to refuge staff, croplands occupy about 486 ha (1,200 ac) at conservation pool. Remaining community types encompass 1,826 ha (4,513 ac) at conservation pool and include grasslands, shelterbelts, and riparian habitat. However, the area of each community was not available.

Of the community types on the refuge, the reservoir (e.g., deepwater habitat) and associated shoreline, cropland, and shelterbelts were not present prior to human settlement. Consequently, the area of native communities on the refuge has been reduced. Further, the grassland and riparian communities, although historically present, have been severely altered floristically and structurally. For example, two plant species that may occur on the refuge (western prairie-fringed orchid and Meads milkweed; scientific names of all species mentioned in this report are given in Appendix B) are listed as threatened or endangered under the Endangered Species Act (ESA) of 1973 (16 U.S.C. 1531-1544, 87 Stat. 884; URL: http:// laws.fws.gov/lawsdigest/esact.html). More detailed information is presented in the section entitled Evaluation of Community Types.

Wildlife Conservation

The 1997 NWRSIA mandates that each refuge develop a CCP that is consistent with the principles of sound fish and wildlife management and available science. Further, this act also specifies that each CCP shall identify and describe the purposes of each refuge; the distribution, migration patterns, and abundance of fish, wildlife, and plant populations and related habitats; significant problems that may adversely affect the populations and habitats of fish, wildlife, and plants and the actions necessary to correct or mitigate such problems; and, to the maximum extent practicable and consistent with this Act, be consistent with fish and wildlife conservation plans of the State in which the refuge is located.

The purpose of this report was not to fully develop information on all species potentially occurring on the refuge. However, some general future direction must be specified with regard to wildlife given the purpose for refuge establishment. Therefore, this report concentrates on the importance of the refuge to migratory birds because these species represent a primary FWS responsibility according to the requirements of the Migratory Bird Treaty Act of 1918 (16 USC 703-711; 40 Stat. 755; URL: http://laws.fws.gov/lawsdigest/migtrea.html). This should not be interpreted as meaning other vertebrates, invertebrates (e.g., butterflies), and plants can be ignored since these organisms are important as individual entities and also because they are critical to proper system function. Rather, information regarding the habitat requirements of these species also should be used in evaluating the direction of future refuge management to ensure that valuable opportunities are not overlooked.

Baseline information on the avian community of Kirwin NWR was developed using a checklist of bird species sighted on the refuge (Igl 1996). Scientific names for all species mentioned are provided in Appendix B; birds follow the American Ornithologists' Union Committee on Classification and Nomenclature (American Ornithologists' Union 1998, 2000, 2002, 2003). In addition, refuge files of duck, goose, and swan counts were used to generate graphs of total annual use days, average annual populations, and average peak populations spanning a 20-year period (Appendix C). There are several qualifying factors that must be considered when considering this information. First, the list from the website represents a composite of all birds that have been sighted over a long time; thus, the list may not accurately represent the current avian community. Second, the list only designates occurrence; thus, the contribution (e.g., source/sink) of the refuge to the species population is not known. Although refuge waterfowl counts contribute information on abundance, it is difficult to compare data among years with any certainty because routes and areas surveyed are not available and likely have varied among years. In addition, count information was not collected based on community type or bird activity. Thus, it was not possible to use this information to determine local use patterns or assess relative importance of different communities. Similarly, the avian list (Appendix B) was not developed using standardized protocols and methods, but based on the long-term refuge bird list, with an additional 29 species added from a research study conducted in the riparian zone on the refuge in the mid-1990s (Sevigny 1998). Regardless of these constraints, this list is valuable because it can help focus discussion among individuals (e.g., FWS personnel, core CCP team) responsible for determining the future management direction of the refuge.

Finally, depending on the source and type of information sought, Kirwin NWR is located in many different regions. In all cases, there is considerable overlap among boundaries although the area encompassed tends to vary greatly. To provide an overall perspective, relevant information regarding species of concern and population targets contained in these plans has been summarized, but no attempt has been made to prioritize or make decisions regarding species or guilds that should receive attention. In some cases, species considered to be of conservation concern at a regional level may not be of concern at a national level, or vice versa. Such differences do not indicate discrepancies; rather, it suggests differences in distribution and population status at different geographical scales. However, the small size of the refuge precludes providing quality habitat for all species and decisions likely will be required to evaluate tradeoffs in management approaches and for development of detailed habitat objectives.

Kirwin National Wildlife Refuge

The refuge bird list includes 233 species, of which 45 are recorded as nesting and four (Piping Plover, Bald Eagle, Whooping Crane, and Least Tern) are listed as threatened or endangered under the ESA. Kirwin NWR also is recognized as a globally Important Bird Area (IBA) by the American Bird Conservancy (URL http://www.abcbirds.org/iba/kansas.htm). The IBA program, initiated by BirdLife International in Europe during the mid-1980's, was developed to recognize and support sites of importance to birds. Based on the criteria developed by BirdLife International, an IBA must maintain and support one or more of the following: (1) species of concern (e.g., threatened and endangered), (2) species with restricted ranges, (3) species vulnerable because of population concentration, and (4) species vulnerable because they occur at high densities due to their congregative behavior (Kushlan et al. 2002).

State of Kansas

Wildlife resources in the state of Kansas were historically rich and varied. Circa 1865, it is estimated that the Great Plains portion of Kansas supported as many as 407 bird species, including about 178 breeding species (Fleharty 1995). Fish and herpetofauna were not as rich due to the paucity of water, but included 30 fish species, 13 amphibian species, and 46 species of reptiles (Fleharty 1995). Although Kirwin NWR is small relative to the geographic area of Kansas, the historic communities composing the refuge likely supported many species mentioned in earlier accounts. Appendix B contains a list of animals and plants known to occur on the refuge.

Bird Conservation Region

Kirwin NWR is located within the Central Mixed-grass Prairie Bird Conservation Region (BCR 19), an ecologically distinct region of 535,734 km^2 (206,848 mi^2) with similar bird communities, habitats, and resource management issues. The area encompassed by BCR 19 extends from the edge of shortgrass prairie on the west to the beginning of tallgrass prairie to the east and includes portions of Texas, Oklahoma, Kansas, and Nebraska (North American Bird Conservation Initiative, URL http://www.nabci-us.org/map.html). Although large areas in this region have been converted to agriculture, areas of high-quality grassland (e.g., Nebraska Sandhills) still remain, including some of the best habitat for the Greater Prairie-Chicken and Henslow's Sparrow, and sandbars along the larger rivers host a large percentage of the continent's breeding Least Tern population. The region also is a spring migration area for the American Avocet, Semipalmated Sandpiper, and Buff-breasted Sandpiper.

Birds of Conservation Concern

The Birds of Conservation Concern (BCC) is the most recent effort to satisfy the 1988 amendment to the Fish and Wildlife Conservation Act, which mandates FWS to "identify species, subspecies, and populations of all migratory nongame birds that, without additional conservation actions, are likely to become candidates for listing under the Endangered Species Act of 1973" (U. S. Fish and Wildlife Service 2002). The document provides species lists at three geographic scales: national, FWS regions, and BCRs. Species considered for inclusion include nongame birds, game birds without hunting seasons, and numerous categories (candidate, proposed endangered or threatened, and recently delisted) used in the ESA. Parameters considered in determining if species within these categories are of concern include population size, extent of range, threats to habitat, and other factors. The BCC should be consulted for details regarding the assessment process.

There are 28 species known to occur on Kirwin NWR that are considered to be of national conservation concern in the BCC (U. S. Fish and Wildlife Service 2002). Among these are 8 shorebirds, 5 hawks and falcons, 2 owls, and 2 sparrows. Twenty-one of these 28 species also are considered to be of conservation concern at either FWS Region 6 or BCR 19 scale (Appendix D). Special note should be made that some species of conservation concern listed for BCR 19 are not on the regional list and, likewise, several species of regional conservation concern were not included in the BCC list for BCR 19 (Appendix D).

North American Waterfowl Management Plan

The national goals set forth in the 1998 update of North American Waterfowl Management Plan (NAWMP) includes (1) maintaining the diversity of duck species throughout North America and achieving a mid-continent breeding population of 39 million ducks during years with average environmental conditions, and (2) reaching or exceeding mid-continent populations for ten individual species, including Gadwall, American Wigeon, Mallard, Blue-winged and Cinnamon Teal, Northern Shoveler, Northern Pintail, Green-winged Teal, Canvasback, Redhead, and Greater and Lesser scaup. These target populations are presented in Appendix D. The plan also establishes population objectives for 30 populations of six goose species, three populations of Trumpeter Swans, and two populations of Tundra Swans. Of these, relevant objectives applicable to Kirwin NWR include reducing all five populations of Canada Geese that migrate through the central flyway and also reducing mid-continent populations of the Snow and Greater White-fronted geese to 1,000,000 and 600,000, respectively. The plan also sets forth objectives to increase the interior population of Trumpeter Swans to 2,500 and reduce the eastern population of Tundra Swans to 80,000 (Appendix D).

Partner's In Flight North American Landbird Conservation Plan

The North American Landbird Conservation Plan (NALCP) is a synthesis of priorities to guide national and international conservation actions targeting 448 native landbirds from 45 families that breed in the United States and Canada (Rich et al. 2004). Each species is assigned scores ranging from 1 (low vulnerability) to 5 (high vulnerability) for 6 factors (population size, breeding distribution, nonbreeding distribution, threats to breeding, threats to nonbreeding, and population trend). These scores subsequently are used to calculate a combined score that represents relative conservation importance (range = 4 [low concern] to 20 [high concern]). Species with a combined score $\geq$ 14, or combined score = 13 and population trend score = 5, are assigned to the Watch List that includes species of highest conservation concern. In addition, a Stewardship List was developed based on avifaunal biomes in North America. These biomes were delineated using cluster analyses to identify groups of BCRs that share similar avifaunas. For each biome, Stewardship Species are those species that have a proportionately high percentage of their world population within a single region during either the breeding or wintering season. Kirwin NWR occurs in the Prairie Avifaunal Biome, which is composed of BCRs 11, 17-19, and 21-23 (Rich et al. 2004). The NALCP should be consulted for details on the scoring and assignment process, national and regional population objectives, and other pertinent information (Rich et al. 2004, URL http://www.partnersinflight.org, URL http://www.rmbo.org/pif/pifdb.html).

The Watch List and Stewardship List of continentally important species in the United States and Canada currently include 100 and 158 species (66 of these species also occur on the Watch List), respectively (Rich et al. 2004). Of these species, two (Greater Prairie-Chicken, Dickcissel) of the Watch List species and five (Mississippi Kite, American Tree Sparrow, Lark Bunting, Grasshopper Sparrow, and Chestnut-collared Longspur) of the Stewardship list species are known to occur on Kirwin NWR (Appendix D). In contrast, there are 21 and seven species of continental importance on the Watch List and Stewardship List in the Prairie Avifaunal Biome, respectively. Of these, two species (Greater Prairie-Chicken and Dickcissel) on the Watch List and six species (Mississippi Kite, American Tree Sparrow, Lark Bunting, Grasshopper Sparrow, Chestnut-collared Longspur, and Lapland Longspur) on the Stewardship List are known to occur on Kirwin NWR.

Shorebird Conservation Region

Kirwin NWR is located in the Central Plains/Playa Lakes Region (CP/PLR) (United States Shorebird Conservation Plan, URL http:// shorebirdplan.fws.gov/RegionalShorebird/ RegionsMap.asp). This region is larger than the area encompassed by BCR 19 and includes portions of Texas, eastern New Mexico and Colorado, western Oklahoma, Kansas, Nebraska, and southeast Wyoming. Thirty-eight shorebird species use habitat in the CP/PLR during migration and 13 of these species also breed in the region (Fellows et al. 2001). Of these, 16 species have been identified as species of primary concern. Based on the Kirwin NWR bird list, 13 of these priority species have been documented on the refuge, including Snowy Plover, Long-billed Curlew, Upland Sandpiper, White-rumped Sandpiper, Baird's Sandpiper, and Piping Plover (Appendix D). The national and regional plans should be consulted for national population objectives, justifications for species designations, and other pertinent information (U. S. Shorebird Conservation Plan, URL http:// shorebirdplan.fws.gov/RegionalShorebird/downloads/ CPPLR.doc).

Waterbird Conservation Region

Kirwin NWR is within the Central Prairies Region of The North American Waterbird Conservation Plan (NAWCP). In North America, separate initiatives exist for waterbirds, shorebirds, and waterfowl. Thus, the NAWCP focuses on seabirds, coastal waterbirds, wading birds, and marsh birds (Waterbird Conservation for the Americas, URL http:// www.waterbirdconservation.org/waterbirds/). There are 23 species listed in the Central Prairies that have been documented on Kirwin NWR. Of these, the conservation status of six species are designated as "not currently at risk", five are considered of "low conservation concern", nine are of "moderate conservation concern", and three are of "high conservation concern" (Kushlan et al. 2002; Appendix D). The entire plan should be consulted to fully understand how scores were determined.

Playa Lakes Joint Venture

At a smaller geographic scale, Kirwin NWR is part of the Playa Lakes Joint Venture (PLJV; URL http:// www.pljv.org/about01.html), which encompasses most of BCR 18 (Shortgrass Prairie) and BCR 19 (Central Mixed-Grass Prairie). Joint ventures originally were conceived by FWS in 1986 to implement the NAWMP. URL http://northamerican.fws.gov/NAWMP/ nawmphp.htm). However, in addition to waterfowl,

many joint ventures (including the PLJV) are now incorporating an "all bird" approach. National and international bird plans provide the foundation for the PLJV master plan, which sets direction for conservation activities within the region. Established in 1989, the mission of the PLJV is to create sustainable landscapes for the benefit of birds, other wildlife, and humans. More specifically, the PLJV directs effort to restore, preserve and protect myriad habitats, including playas, saline lakes, riparian areas, and grasslands for resident, wintering, migrating, and breeding birds. More than 400 species of birds use the PLJV, including continentally important populations of waterfowl, shorebirds, other waterbirds, and grassland birds. The objectives established for the PLJV in the 1998 update to the NAWMP are to restore and enhance 4,047 ha (10,000 ac) and 10,117 ha (25,000 ac) of habitat, respectively, and protect 20,639 ha (51,000 ac) of existing habitat.

Community Types

This section has been divided based on general community designations. This was done to improve clarity, but it should be recognized that such distinctions are arbitrary. Communities do not occur as distinct entities but grade together as evidenced by the movement of nutrients, energy, and wildlife within and among communities. Therefore, information for one community may be relevant for other communities. Attempts were made to identify these relationships, but some may have been overlooked.

For each community, a brief history is provided on historic and current conditions and potential concerns and opportunities are identified. The inclusion of historic information is not intended as an effort to direct refuge management toward restoring presettlement conditions. Rather, historic descriptions have been incorporated because they can provide valuable insight regarding the original location, extent, and vegetation composition of communities and changes in abiotic factors (e.g., hydrology) that have occurred through time. Together with information on current conditions, historic descriptions can be used to (1) identify important changes in processes that may require further evaluation and (2) better understand the potential of refuge lands.

Reservoir (Deepwater)
Historically, there was no deepwater habitat on the area that now constitutes the refuge. Flows from the North Fork Solomon River and Bow Creek flowed unimpeded through refuge lands and occasionally inundated the floodplain during wet periods. Construction of Kirwin Reservoir has changed these conditions. Obviously, damming the flows of the Solomon River and Bow Creek and impounding water in the historic floodplain of the rivers created deepwater habitat. The surface acreage of the reservoir varies dramatically from about 2,024 ha (5,000 ac) at conservation pool (527.7 m [1731.25 ft] elevation) to 356 ha (879 ac) during drought periods (refuge staff). During the site visit the reservoir elevation was 522.9 m (1715.6 ft), but water is expected to drop an additional 3.4 m (11 ft) in the summer of 2003 (refuge staff). These fluctuations likely are due to a combination of frequent drought periods coupled with upstream pumping from the aquifer (U.S. Bureau of Reclamation 2002). Since the mid-1960's, inflows to Kirwin Reservoir have declined significantly as evidenced by a long-term reduction in average annual inflow of 3,577 ha-m (29,000 ac-ft) between 1920-1964 (6,562 ha-m [53,200 ac-ft]) and 1965-1999 (4,070 ha-m [33,000 ac-ft]; U.S. Bureau of Reclamation 2002). In addition, >150 alluvial wells occur above the refuge (U.S. Bureau of Reclamation 2002). The majority of these wells are for agricultural uses, but municipal wells also exist.

There also have been less obvious influences. Prior to settlement, some amount of sediment was transported from the uplands to the channel during storm events. The amount of sediment varied, but intact upland and floodplain vegetation probably reduced the amount of sediment that entered the channel. Following settlement, increased agricultural activity likely altered the amount and pattern of sediment transport and deposition in the valley. More than 50% of the basin is currently cropland (U.S. Bureau of Reclamation 1984) and cultivation and intensive grazing in some areas (e.g., areas with large topographic relief) have likely increased the amount of erosion, and therefore sediment, entering the floodplain. Prior to constructing reservoirs in the Solomon Basin, the distribution of this sediment varied depending on antecedent conditions and magnitude of the current event. Following construction, however, the dams functioned as a barrier to sediment transport downstream. Thus, although sediment deposition can occur at various locations upstream of Kirwin Dam, the dam itself now represents a terminal location that likely traps the majority of sediment that enters the reservoir.

The potential impacts of increased sedimentation at one location are numerous. In terms of quantity, sediment is the major pollutant of wetlands, lakes, estuaries, and reservoirs in the United States (Baker 1992). Sediment quality also is an environmental concern because sediment may act as both a sink and source for water-quality constituents (U. S. Geological Survey, URL http://ks.water.usgs.gov/Kansas/ studies/ressed/). Once in the food chain, sediment-derived constituents may bioaccumulate and pose an even greater concern to fish, wildlife, and humans. In addition, sediment loads may never consolidate with bottom materials. The surface waters in the basin of the North Fork Solomon River are reported as turbid with moderate to high concentrations of dissolved solids (U.S. Bureau of Reclamation 2002). Thus, increased sedimentation may increase turbidity even more due to wind and wave action that periodically suspends sediment throughout the water column. This could lead to other impacts, including reduced dissolved oxygen concentrations, altered nutrient availability, and reduced sunlight penetration. If sufficient, these changes can eliminate or reduce growth of submerged aquatic vegetation (SAV) (Robel 1961, Kullberg 1974, Dieter 1990).

The extent that sediment impacts have occurred, or potentially could occur, in Kirwin Reservoir has received attention recently. In 1998, the BOR initiated a sampling program to assess the presence or absence of organic and inorganic compounds in reservoir waters. Part of this study involved collecting two groups of four sediment cores near the dam (Christensen 1999). Sediment thickness estimated from these cores ranged from 2.9-3.4 m (9.5-11.3 ft) in the first group of 4 cores to 2.1-2.3 m (6.9-7.4 ft) in the second group. Unfortunately, it was not possible to accurately determine sedimentation rates due to core shortening (i.e., essentially a partial collapse or compression of the core that prevented accurate dating). However, a visual examination of the cores revealed thick layers of sediment in the deepest intervals, which indicates sediment deposition was greater in the early years of the reservoir. This is consistent with other reservoir studies (Ritchie et al. 1986; Callendar and Robbins 1993) that have demonstrated decreased sedimentation rates with reservoir age. Historical stream flow data indicate that much of the early sediment deposition in the reservoir may have been caused by floods during the 1957 and 1960 water years (Christensen 1999).

Another objective of the BOR sampling program was to determine potential environmental effects due to elevated levels of total organic carbon (TOC), trace metals, and major nutrients. The Environmental Protection Agency has established two threshold concentrations for many of these elements. The threshold effect level (TEL) is assumed to represent the concentration below which toxic effects rarely occur, whereas the probable effect level (PEL) indicates the concentration that usually or frequently results in toxicity. Adverse effects occasionally occur at concentrations between the TEL and PEL. Both the TEL and PEL are guidelines used to screen for possible hazardous chemical levels, but are not regulatory criteria.

Total organic carbon was measured because various organic solutes can form complexes that affect metal solubility (Hem 1992). The median TOC concentration in the reservoir was 11,600 mg/kg and the trend was not increasing. There are no published TEL and PEL limits for TOC; thus, the impact of existing levels is not readily apparent. However, further investigation should be conducted to obtain information from other reservoir studies to ascertain potential impacts of current TOC levels.

Selenium (Se) is a naturally occurring trace element common in the marine shales underlying the Solomon River Basin (see section on Geology). This metal is of concern because irrigation in other areas underlain by marine shales has resulted in elevated Se concentrations that have caused birth defects, reproductive failure, and death in fish and wildlife (U.S. Bureau of Reclamation 2002). No TEL or PEL has been established for Se, but concentrations ≥ 4.0 mg/kg in sediment can result in bioaccumulation in fish and wildlife (Lemly and Smith 1987). Concentrations of Se in Kirwin Reservoir bottom-sediment ranged from <0.3 to 2.2 mg/kg, indicating low potential for bioaccumulation (Christensen 1999). However, Se did exhibit a significant increasing trend ($P = 0.006$) in one of the two cores, suggesting that concentrations may be of concern in the future.

Reports by Christensen (1999) and Christensen and Juracek (2001) also indicate median arsenic (As) concentrations (range = 4.6-10.0 mg/kg) exceeded the TEL (7.24 mg/kg) but not the PEL (41.6 mg/kg) established for this element. However, a significant increasing As trend was not evident. Arsenic could originate from many potential sources, including underlying geologic features (Christensen and Juracek 2001) or pesticides and industrial activities (Pais and Jones 1997). However, industrial sources are not likely

given the predominance of agriculture in the basin (Christensen and Juracek 2001). The median concentration of copper also exceeded the TEL (18.7 mg/kg) as did cadmium in four samples. In contrast, chromium, lead, nickel, silver, zinc, and mercury either were not detected or did not exceed TEL limits. These results clearly indicate that subsequent monitoring of heavy metals and other water quality parameters are warranted. Although no significant effects have been documented, potential for future issues may arise given evidence of increasing trends for some metals.

Phosphorous (P) and nitrogen (N) are nutrients required for plant growth, but excessive amounts can enter reservoirs from fertilizer runoff or other non-point pollution sources and create problems. The median P and N concentration in core samples from Kirwin was 616 mg/kg and 1,700 mg/kg, respectively. However, only P exhibited a significant increasing trend. Although no TEL and PEL limits have been established for P and N, additional information could be obtained to better understand potential impacts. For example, excessive P has been shown to cause algal blooms that can reduce dissolved oxygen concentrations and cause fish mortality, or reduce light penetration to levels that prevent growth of some aquatic plant species. Information regarding nutrient levels that result in algal blooms, or cause other changes in aquatic biota (e.g., plants, animal) could be used to develop desired thresholds. Although reservoir water levels are managed by the BOR, it may be possible for FWS to recommend or help establish water quality criteria that would ensure the needs of fish and wildlife are met.

Published information on the type and amount of SAV in the reservoir was not located during the initial literature search and the refuge staff was unable to provide any qualitative observations. This is unfortunate because plant composition and biomass occurring in the deepwater community greatly influences potential wildlife values. Plants capable of growing in deep water provide substrate for invertebrates (Krull 1970, Voigts 1976) that, in combination with plant parts, provide foods for many different vertebrates (e.g., fish, waterbirds). In contrast, if SAV is not present, the deepwater community may only provide roosting and loafing habitat for birds. To better evaluate this community, additional searches for information on plant resources should be pursued, including contact with personnel from Kansas Department of Wildlife and Parks and BOR to obtain any reports or documents that may exist.

Waterfowl counts conducted between 1983 and 2001 document ducks, geese, and swans occurring on the refuge in varying numbers (Appendix C). On an annual basis, the primary periods of use occur during spring and fall migration; however, some species, primarily Canada Geese and Mallards, remain on the refuge during some winters (Appendix C, U.S. Bureau of Reclamation 2002). Both diving ducks and geese use the deepwater portion of the reservoir. Plant composition and biomass information is lacking; thus, it is not possible to determine if foraging habitat is available. Waterfowl surveys only provide weekly estimates on the entire refuge. Information on numbers and activities (e.g., foraging, resting) of each species in individual habitat types (e.g., deepwater versus shoreline) are lacking. Therefore, this data cannot be used to speculate on the type and availability of resources and it is impossible to arrive at any definitive conclusions. However, at a minimum it is likely that the deepwater community provides roosting and loafing habitat for waterfowl (ducks, geese, swans), as well as sanctuary from shooting during hunting season (U.S. Bureau of Reclamation 2002). This zone also could provide additional benefits in the form of foraging habitat if SAV beds or invertebrates are present. The types of foraging habitat available would largely depend on the types and locations of food items. For example, the presence of pondweed drupelets or invertebrates within about 46 cm (18 in) of the water surface is available for dabbling ducks, whereas swans can access pondweed foliage at greater depths (Fredrickson and Reid 1986, Fredrickson and Laubhan 1994).

Based on conversations with refuge staff, another interesting issue that would merit further investigation is the value of the deepwater zone as refuge during the hunting season. Currently, this area is closed to hunting and the staff thinks this increases the number and duration of time that geese are in the area. A competing idea is that goose numbers near the refuge are positively correlated with the amount of row crops. Sufficient data may be available to conduct a correlation analysis between the size and availability of the closed zone, cropland acres, and goose numbers. Although correlation analysis is only a "measure of association" and does not prove cause-and-effect, this analysis may provide some insight or help identify variables to monitor in the future.

Management Potential -The ability of FWS to manage the deepwater habitat is minimal. Reservoir elevations are determined by other federal entities that must consider several factors (e.g., irrigation, flood control) other than wildlife. Hydrology, including the direction, magnitude, and time of water level fluctuations, is the primary factor influencing resource production and availability (Mitsch and Gosselink 1993, Fredrickson and Laubhan 1994). The inability of FWS to influence these hydrologic parameters prevents the ability to reliably stimulate or maintain desired plant communities and associated food resources, or influence resource availability (e.g., water depth between food resources and water surface). Even if FWS could establish guidelines specifically for wildlife, the dramatic fluctuations in surface area caused by uncontrollable factors (e.g., precipitation, upstream groundwater pumping) would make it difficult to reliably and consistently achieve desired outcomes.

Although direct management is minimal, the deepwater community still provides resources that contribute to the overall value of the refuge. Therefore, FWS should consider options that can be used to indirectly influence the values that are provided as a result of annual reservoir operation. Potential options to consider include working cooperatively with BOR to establish water quality criteria and continuing to maintain existing agreements that designate a portion of the deepwater community as a closed area during hunting.

Shoreline
The shoreline and deepwater communities are both part of the reservoir and, therefore, are functionally connected both spatially and temporally. They also share some of the same ecological attributes, including source and quality of water. However, these communities have been separated because they are very different with respect to some hydrologic parameters (e.g., water depth), plant communities, and wildlife resources.

Definitions vary, but the shoreline community is defined in this report as the portion of the reservoir (excluding the riparian zone) with water depths that range from saturated soils to <61 cm (24 in). The general shape of the shoreline is linear, but the width, and spatial position of this area change both annually and seasonally depending on reservoir water levels and bathymetry (i.e., topography of reservoir bottom sediments). For example, the bathymetry of the shoreline has been differentially influenced by erosion following reservoir impoundment. The presence of deep and shallow cutbacks caused by wave action can significantly influence habitat suitability for some species that tolerate a narrow range of water depths (e.g., shorebirds). The paucity of palustrine wetlands on the refuge means that the shoreline is the only community that potentially can provide substantial foraging habitat for dabbling ducks (unless SAV occurs in the deepwater community), shorebirds, and wading birds. However, a sufficient area of suitable (e.g., proper substrate, water depth) shoreline must be available if the community is to provide limiting resources (aquatic invertebrates, seeds, tubers) in quantities that benefit different waterbird guilds.

Although area estimates of the shoreline community were not available, the bathymetry and water level data needed to develop estimates is likely available from the BOR. The use of this data to develop curves for estimating shoreline area is highly recommended because it would likely prove useful in future discussions regarding management potential and values of this community. For example, the range of water depths along the shore at different elevations could be compared to water depths used by foraging waterbirds to determine area of suitable habitat available. In addition, the refuge staff reported that an agreement exists between certain entities to maintain conservation pool at 527.7 m (1731.30 ft), rather than the legal elevation of 527.1 m (1729.25 ft). The potential impacts (positive or negative) of this increase on available foraging habitat for various avian guilds could be estimated using the above mentioned curves, but would be difficult otherwise.

Because area is important, a coarse estimate of 91-271 ha (224-670 ac) for the shoreline community at conservation pool was derived to provide some perspective. The accuracy of this estimate should be viewed with extreme skepticism for several reasons. First, the estimate uses an assumed average width of 15-46 m (50-150 ft). Exact widths are unknown and likely vary extensively around the perimeter of the reservoir. Second, the estimate is based on a shoreline length of 60 km (37 mi) at conservation pool which likely includes portions of the shoreline that would be more appropriately considered the riparian community. Also, and perhaps most important, fluctuations in the reservoir surface are known to be dramatic. Consequently, a single estimate at conservation pool does not capture the full range of shoreline area that occurs within and among years. However, this estimate does suggest that the area of shoreline is sufficient to warrant further consideration.

The shoreline potentially can provide unique resources for a diverse array of avifauna. According to refuge files, Double-crested Cormorants and Great Blue Herons have nested on the refuge since 1952 and 1963, respectively. Reproductive effort varies annually, but between 1960 and 1995 the number of Great Blue Heron nests has ranged from 1-20 with production of 2-90 young. During the same period, Double-crested Cormorant nests and young have ranged from 3-37 and 40-60, respectively. The current location of rookeries occurs within, or adjacent to, the shoreline community near the main reservoir body in the eastern portion of the refuge. Trees currently used for nesting appear to be adjacent to stream channels that were inundated when water was impounded by the reservoir. Many of these trees were killed as a result of high water in the 1990's, but many remain standing and still provide suitable nesting habitat.

In addition, Least Terns occasionally nest within the shoreline community and protection of ground nests is required. Exposed sandbars constitute the preferred nesting substrate of Least Terns. However, substrates similar to sandbars are exposed along the shoreline when reservoir elevation recedes and some Least Terns occasionally nest in these areas.

The primary value of the shoreline community, based on the geographic location of the refuge, likely is foraging habitat for a variety of waterbirds. This area constitutes a zone of high biological productivity. The growth of plants during drawdown results in the production of food resources (e.g., seeds, tubers) and the release of nutrients when vegetation decomposes upon reflooding can be assimilated by small aquatic organisms (e.g., microinvertebrates) (Fredrickson and Laubhan 1994). These organisms constitute the forage base for macroinvertebrates, fish, and amphibians, which are the primary foods of many waterbirds. In addition, the hydrologic fluctuations that occur within this area create numerous microhabitats that can be used by numerous species.

Herons and other wading birds forage primarily on aquatic animals, including fish, amphibians, and macroinvertebrates. Although some species are capable of capturing prey in water >60 cm (24 in), the majority of foraging typically occurs within the shoreline community (e.g., shallow water or along the water-mud interface) (Fredrickson and Reid 1986). Except for extreme fluctuations, changes in reservoir levels likely do not alter production or availability of fish, the primary food item of these species (but see Gawlik 2002 for impacts that can occur given the right circumstances). During drought years, it is conceivable that fish kills may occur. This may or may not impact foraging efficiency and nest success of waders depending on the biomass of foods that remain during these periods. Although pertinent data was not located during this initial investigation, Kansas Department of Wildlife and Parks may have relevant information.

Ducks (diving and dabbling) and shorebirds also forage within the shoreline community (Fredrickson and Reid 1986, Skagen and Knopf 1994). In fact, the paucity of palustrine wetlands suggests that these species rely almost exclusively on the shoreline for foraging when using the refuge. However, refuge survey data does not provide information to confirm this assumption. Further, the production and availability of resources for these species is difficult to predict because of the dynamic water fluctuations that occur in this edge community. For example, during March 2003 vegetation along the northern shoreline included reed canary grass, saltcedar, and Canada thistle. There also were extensive areas of bare ground. Although the production of foods (browse, seeds, tuber, etc.) for ducks and geese appears minimal, the growing season had not yet started and additional plants may germinate. If additional germination does not occur, the extensive areas of unvegetated shoreline likely will provide foraging habitat for spring migrant shorebirds. However, optimum foraging depths vary among shorebirds depending on size (i.e., tarsus length); thus, not all shorebirds would benefit equally. In contrast, a very different plant community was evident during a field visit to the refuge in 1999. This visit was conducted during the growing season and water levels were much higher. My field notes indicate minimal bare ground and the presence of smartweed, millet, bulrushes, cattail, beggarticks, ricecut grass, spikerush, cocklebur, sedges, and panic grass among other species. Depending on fall water conditions, the shoreline would have provided excellent foraging habitat for dabbling ducks and geese due to the large biomass of seeds and browse produced. In contrast, shorebird foraging habitat would likely have been minimal due to excessive vegetation cover.

The above observations fromt two different years provide evidence that the seed bank within the shoreline community is diverse and includes both desirable (e.g., browse, seed-bearing) and undesirable (e.g., invasive, exotic) plant species. The species that germinate from the seed bank, and the ultimate densities of species that survive, are determined by a multitude of factors. Most species that germinate in the shoreline area require substrates that are moist to wet, but not flooded (van der Valk and Davis 1978). Thus, the most important factor controlling germination likely is the annual changes in reservoir water levels, including the magnitude, timing, and rate of water level fluctuations. These hydrologic parameters greatly influence recruitment from the seed bank by affecting time of soil exposure, soil temperature and oxygen levels, and the rate of soil moisture loss (Leck 1989, Fredrickson 1991). Water quality also may be important because constituents (e.g., salts, iron, copper) in the water are bound by soil particles at the soil-water interface and can affect plant germination and growth. This deserves further investigation because of water quality issues in the reservoir. However, the diversity of plants that have already been documented along the shoreline suggests that water quality currently is not severely impacting the germination or survival capability of many species.

Management Potential – Similar to the deepwater portion of the reservoir, the ability of FWS to manage the shoreline community is constrained by the lack of hydrologic control. Consequently, the value of the shoreline community to waterbirds likely will vary among species and years. Trees adjacent to the reservoir and the presence of fish near the shoreline are probably consistently available. Thus, suitable habitat for breeding Great Blue Herons and Double-crested Cormorants, as well as migrating and wintering Bald Eagles, is usually present on the refuge in most years. In contrast, foraging habitat for ducks and shorebirds will be more variable for two primary reasons. First, it is not possible to manipulate water levels to match the germination requirements of plants that produce a large biomass of foods (e.g., seeds, tubers, browse) and provide substrate for invertebrates. Second, water levels cannot be intentionally manipulated to coincide with duck and shorebird migration periods. Therefore, in the absence of hydrologic control, some exposed and vegetated shoreline habitat will be available to shorebirds and ducks every year, but water level changes that expose abundant foods during migration will occur only sporadically. Finally, the availability of habitat for Least Terns varies, but likely is more predictable than ducks and shorebirds. This statement is based on the reported long-term drought/wet cycle of 30 years with about 23 years of drought and seven years of wet conditions (refuge staff). According to the refuge staff, reservoir pool elevations tend to consistently decrease during the drought phase. When this occurs, the availability of substrates suitable for Least Tern nesting tends to become more reliable, and the probability of nest destruction due to flooding less likely, during a period of several years. During the start of the wet period, water levels in the reservoir start to increase, and, if nesting is attempted, the likelihood of nests being destroyed by flooding increases.

Another reality is the potential for an unfavorable plant community to develop in the shoreline community. The land-water interface in this zone is a prime area for the establishment and proliferation of many invasive species due to the frequent presence of exposed soil, variable soil moisture, and high nutrient availability. For example, along the north shoreline numerous saltcedar seedlings and stems of Canada thistle and reed canary grass were evident. Although currently present only in small numbers, the potential exists for expansion of these invasive species (or others) along the shoreline, which could result in the loss of current shoreline values (Sudbrock 1993, Bailey et al. 2001). Evidence of this potential exists in the floodplain of the lower riparian zone where reed canary grass and Canada thistle currently dominate the herbaceous vegetation (see below).

FWS cannot alter the hydrology of the reservoir to minimize the potential for invasions of non-natives to occur. Similarly, FWS cannot intentionally raise pool elevation to eliminate invasions that do occur. Nevertheless, the refuge staff is responsible for addressing invasive species that do occur. Potential control options (herbicides, fire, mechanical equipment) exist, but implementation may not be possible in some years (e.g., too wet). Also, many techniques often are costly and require repeated application to be successful. Thus, it is recommended that decisions be made regarding the ability and/or desire to conduct such operations under different conditions. Information available in the literature and refuge files should be adequate to develop working hypotheses of potential tradeoffs (e.g., costs, benefits, probability of success) related to active management in this community. This information should be consolidated prior to CCP development.

In summary, the shoreline community has the potential to provide many values to waterbirds that other communities on the refuge do not provide. There also is potential for extensive, rapid colonization of invasive species. These detrimental impacts are common on many reservoirs, and approaches to minimize impacts are often difficult to develop due to constraints imposed by the reservoir operation plan. In the case of Kirwin Reservoir, the only recommendation is to consult with the BOR to determine if annual operations can be altered slightly to take advantage of existing conditions that occur in some years. For example, it is likely that the release of a relatively small volume of water in spring would expose a large amount of shoreline habitat around the reservoir for spring migrant shorebirds. Such releases would not have to occur annually; rather, an agreement could be developed that would result in release only when pool elevations are above a certain level. In many cases, such alterations may have only negligible impacts on other reservoir uses but result in significant wildlife benefits.

Riparian
The riparian community, which includes the floodplain and channel of the Solomon River and Bow Creek, was dynamic historically. Although both streams were considered perennial (Leonard 1952), flows were highly variable depending on precipitation cycles.

Stream hydrology was characterized by flood flows in the spring and low flows or ponding during the summer and fall (U.S. Bureau of Reclamation 2002). These extremes in hydrology influenced the types of flora that developed and the fauna that inhabited the riparian system. During major floods the channel was reworked, vegetation was uprooted, and sediment was transported downstream and deposited at various locations in the channel and floodplain. These actions resulted in the creation of various channel habitats (e.g., pools, riffles), marsh areas adjacent to the rivers, and sites for regeneration and growth of various plant types in the floodplain.

The historic floristic composition of the floodplain included grasses, forbs, and woody vegetation. Kuchler (1974) described this community as "floodplain forest and savanna", with scattered trees and shrubs and a dominant ground cover of bluestem prairie. However, he also states that "the prairie was suppressed in areas of dense woody growth", suggesting that certain areas of the floodplain were extensively forested. The wooded component apparently was continuous but narrow based on accounts of early settlers and one aerial photograph (Plate 5, page 18 in Leonard 1952) of the Solomon River near Glade, Kansas. Dominant woody species included cottonwood, American elm, hackberry, and peachleaved willow, whereas the dominant herbaceous vegetation consisted of big bluestem, little bluestem, switchgrass, and Indian grass. In contrast, marshes were dominated by prairie cordgrass and lesser numbers of myriad species, including bulrushes, cattail, and rice cutgrass (Kuchler 1974).

The historic wildlife community inhabiting the riparian community was diverse and unique. Forests were rare in the Great Plains and the woody vegetation provided cover, forage, and nesting substrates for neotropical migrants that were not available in other communities. The tall grasses provided important resources for both migratory and resident wildlife, and marshes provided resources for a host of waterfowl. The stream fishery was not rich and included only species (e.g., plains killifish, red shiner, creek chub) that could tolerate extremes in hydroperiod, temperature, current velocity, and dissolved oxygen concentrations (U.S. Bureau of Reclamation 2002).

However, as with other communities on the refuge, human settlement and the accompanying changes have greatly altered processes and influenced vegetation in the riparian community. Among the most important changes include reservoir construction, increased groundwater pumping, diversion dam construction, and irrigation canal development (Christensen and Juracek 2001). The potential range of impacts caused by these changes varies from subtle to obvious depending on the year and antecedent environmental conditions. The upper portion of the riparian community differs greatly from the lower portion due to the impacts of the above-mentioned changes.

In the mid-1990's, the floodplains of both streams supported trees on the refuge, but the width varied from a few scattered trees to areas as wide as 180 m (590 ft) (Sevigny 1998). Of the nine river systems in the western two-thirds of Kansas, the amount of woody riparian vegetation on the Solomon River (3,112 ha [7,689 ac]) ranked second only to the Lower Arkansas (5,083 ha [12,560 ac]) (Eddy 1994). The composition of trees in the mid-1990's was dominated by eastern cottonwood (58%) and willow (25%) with lesser amounts of American elm (4%) and green ash (3%), hackberry, boxelder, and mulberry (Sevigny 1998, Eddy 1994). The shrub and vine component (5%) also was evident, but some non-native trees have invaded the system, including saltcedar (Eddy 1994), Siberian elm, and honey locust (Sevigny 1998, refuge staff). Perhaps the greatest change from historic structure and composition has occurred in the ground vegetation. The once dominant tall, warm season grasses described by Kuchler (1974) have been replaced by shorter cool season grasses (e.g., smooth brome), which has altered structural and floristic diversity (refuge staff, personal observation).

The avian community also remains diverse, which is not surprising. The ability of riparian systems to support a diverse assemblage of vertebrates is well documented (Pashley et al. 2000). However, the composition and relative abundance of species have likely changed due to landscape level changes in land use (e.g., agriculture). In 1997, a study of the riparian bird community on the refuge during spring migration resulted in the identification 87 species from 19 families (Sevigny 1998). A detailed inspection of this list identified some intriguing (although not substantiated) aspects that may be related to changes in ground flora. The nine most abundant species (>100 recorded) were the House Wren, Blue Jay, Black-capped Chickadee, Mourning Dove, Northern Cardinal, Common Yellowthroat, Red-winged Blackbird, and Brown-headed Cowbird. Based on Breeding Bird Survey (BBS) data for Region 6 of FWS, the Black-capped Chickadee (n = 257 routes, trend = 0.9, P = 0.19, 95% confidence interval [CI] = -0.4 – 2.1), Mourning Dove (n = 568 routes, trend = 0.0, P = 0.82, 95% CI = -0.4 – 0.5), Northern Cardinal (n = 73 routes, trend = 1.1, P = 0.06, 95% CI = 0.0 – 2.2), Common Yellowthroat (n = 322 routes, trend = 0.1, P = 0.89, 95% CI = -0.8 – 0.9), Red-winged Blackbird (n = 525 routes, trend = 0.1, P = 0.84, 95% CI = -0.5 – 0.6), and Brown-headed Cowbird (n = 533 routes, trend = 0.1, P = 0.71, 95% CI = -0.4 – 0.6) exhibited stable populations trends, whereas the House Wren (n = 410 routes, trend = 2.4, P = 0.00, 95% CI = 1.8 – 3.1) and Blue Jay (n = 179 routes, trend = 0.8, P = 0.02, 95% CI = 0.1 – 1.6), exhibited increasing population trends between 1966 and 2003 (Sauer et al. 2004, URL http://www.mbr-pwrc.usgs.gov/bbs/bbs.html). Further, most of these species are capable of adapting to changes occurring in the riparian communities throughout the western United States (Saab 1999). In contrast, however, the list also included 19 species whose status is of some concern according to current regional and national plans (Appendix D). The presence of these species in low abundance suggests the riparian plant community has not been completely altered, but subtle, significant changes have occurred that has reduced habitat suitability for some species. Additional investigation to identify these changes and their causes would be valuable for determining appropriate future management actions. However, given the impacts of high water during the mid-1990's (see below) the preceding statement only applies to the upper portion of the riparian community.

Comparing shifts in avian communities between historic and current periods often is used as a technique to describe community changes. This approach has much value, but it also has several weaknesses. First, this technique cannot identify all changes that potentially have occurred. Second, changes in processes often can only be detected by certain avian parameters (e.g., abundance, nest density); thus, multiple parameters often must be collected and this data is rarely available in historic accounts. Finally, these comparisons only illustrate past trends and do not identify cause-effect relationships. Consequently, they provide little information on future expectations, particularly in environments that are subject to rapid and extreme changes due to human events (see below).

To remedy this shortcoming, information regarding change in processes that influence community structure and function also must be developed. Traditionally, ecologists assumed that the most important processes affecting populations operated at local spatial scales (Carothers et al. 1974, Urban and Smith 1989). Recent research, however, has indicated that larger scale assessment also should be considered (Wiens 1989, Forman 1995). These large scale assessments can help (1) identify changes that are preventing desired conditions from being obtained, (2) identify future management actions that are likely to be most effective, and (3) determine if management is feasible or warranted. Often, as is the case with the riparian community, the evaluation largely is subjective because all the required information is not available. However, a combination of available information integrated with logic and general principles of how processes affect community structure and function can still provide valuable insight for making management decisions. The following information has been developed based on this perspective.

Increased groundwater pumping, canals, diversion dams, and reservoir construction have all contributed to altered stream flow in both streams (Christensen and Juracek 2001). However, the impacts to the riparian community caused by pumping, diversion dams and canals differ in some ways from those caused by the reservoir and will be discussed separately. The first three activities occur above the refuge, are associated largely with agriculture, and have changed the annual hydrograph by reducing the volume of water in the channel and changing the timing of peak and low periods (Wis. Bureau of Reclamation 2002).

Exact shifts should be determined by analyzing long-term hydrographs (if available). However, compared to historic conditions, the general effect is that larger storm events or longer wet periods are required to cause the same amount of overbank flooding and channel scouring. The periodic occurrence of these actions is critical to maintaining channel diversity (e.g., pools, riffles) and creating conditions suitable for germination of new woody and herbaceous vegetation. In addition, the long-term average depth to the water table underlying the floodplain has likely increased. This change has occurred because the groundwater in the floodplain is in direct connection with water in the channel (see sections on Geology and Groundwater). In general, these two entities are in dynamic quilibrium. Due to upstream influences, the volume, and therefore depth, of water in the channel has decreased during non-flood periods. As water depth has decreased, free water (i.e., not bound by soil particles) in the ground has likely seeped into the channel until equilibrium is reached or no more groundwater is available. The greater the drop in channel water depth (e.g., during extreme drought), the more likely groundwater will seep into the channel. Ultimately, these changes can result in decreased soil moisture in the rooting zone of the floodplain. This can impact plant community composition and structure because altered soil moisture can influence germination potential of seeds and affect the growth of existing plants. Site-specific information necessary to confirm these changes and determine if the magnitude of change has been sufficient to alter plant composition is not available, but it is recommended that data be collected. This can be accomplished by refuge staff using relatively inexpensive methods and would be valuable in determining future management actions.

Construction of the reservoir occurred immediately downstream of the riparian community managed by the refuge. Similar to upstream hydrologic alterations, the dam has reduced flow velocity in the stream because water no longer can be transported downstream unobstructed. Historically, these events were important because floodplain vegetation was disturbed and areas suitable for new germination were created. The reduced frequency or absence of these events likely lowers the potential of bare, moist substrate necessary for regeneration of species such as cottonwood and willow (Scott et al. 1993). In addition, the reservoir functions to store water during wet years. During prolonged wet periods, or during extreme precipitation events, the impoundment of floodwaters can result in inundation of the floodplain to deeper depths and for longer periods than historically occurred. If inundation lasts a sufficient time it can lead to the mortality of vegetation (Teskey and Hinckley 1977). Also, the release of water from the reservoir is timed to coincide with irrigation needs, usually summer and early fall (U.S. Bureau of Reclamation 2002). This, in combination with upstream activities, has changed the period of maximum stream flow from spring to summer. This shift has several impacts, but one of the most important is the potential effect on germination of riparian vegetation. Seeds of many species, including cottonwood and willow, are dispersed in spring, are short-lived, and require bare, moist substrate for germination. Thus, the shift from spring to summer flows can negatively impact germination of these species.

During certain years, or combinations of years, the effect of these impacts can result in severe and long-lasting effects on riparian vegetation. This is obvious based on the damage to riparian vegetation caused by the most recent wet period (1993-2000). This damage was still evident in March 2003 and illustrates potential management issues that should be addressed during CCP development. A general chronological description of events follows:

1. A period of high water starts in 1993 with a 140 cm (55 in) rain event (U.S. Bureau of Reclamation 2002, refuge staff). The riparian study (Sevigny 1998) was being conducted at about this time.

2. Water levels in the reservoir increase enough to back water into the lower portion of the riparian zone immediately upstream of the reservoir.

3. The water remains at depths long enough in the lower portion to kill all but 142 ha (350 ac) of riparian vegetation (U. S. Fish and Wildlife Service 1996). Although mortality was not as evident in the upper riparian zone, it is likely that this area was also impacted to some extent. For example, water in the upper channel could not be evacuated downstream until water was released from the reservoir. Thus, some of the same plant species (e.g., reed canary grass, Canada thistle) that became established in the lower riparian zone also became established in low elevation portions of the upper zone.

4. The wet period ends in 2000 and water recedes between 2001 and 2003. To facilitate crop irrigation downstream, releases occur primarily during summer months (U.S. Bureau of Reclamation 2002).

5. The release of water is slow and scouring does not occur in either the channel or floodplain.

6. Germination of woody vegetation is minimal because bare, moist substrate is not available during spring when seeds of cottonwood and willow disperse from surviving parent trees.

7. Germination of herbaceous plants occurs, but species composition is dominated by reed canary grass and Canada thistle. This is expected since seeds and rhizomes of these species are adapted to growth in moist, warm soils that frequently occur with summer removal of water.

8. In the spring of 2003, the floodplain consists of standing, dead timber with an understory of Canada thistle and reed canary grass.

This scenario likely occurs infrequently based on the fact that it has occurred only once since reservoir construction in 1952. This is not surprising based on

information provided by the refuge staff that the long-term drought/wet cycle spans a 30-year period with about 23 years of drought and seven years of wet conditions. Because the most recent wet period (1993-2000) ended three years ago, reservoir water levels should continue to decline over the next 20 years. However, even if these long-term predictions are correct, the impacts of recent high water have been severe. Tree mortality has been significant, regeneration of the woody component is sparse, and non-native vegetation has replaced natives in the understory. Undoubtedly, such changes have also altered the avian community from what was reported in the mid-1990's. Perhaps more important, restoration will be costly in terms of both money and labor. Some of the dead timber may have to be removed, the invasive species controlled, and suitable conditions for regeneration of desirable trees and grasses created. Therefore, it is recommended that more information be obtained regarding the relationship between reservoir pool elevations and the duration and depth of floodplain inundation for different reaches of the riparian community. This would help in determining the potential costs, benefits, and reliability of managing different portions of the riparian community. Several techniques could be used to develop information on flooding depth in the floodplain. The most comprehensive (e.g., full range of estimates) and accurate technique would involve the use of bathymetry or topographic data that encompasses both the reservoir and tributary streams. Alternatively, current aerial photographs of the reservoir at different pool elevations could be used to estimate relationships. Data on flood frequency and duration can be developed based on the number of times and duration the reservoir pool exceeded certain elevations, respectively.

Management Potential – Streams, and their associated floodplains, are complex ecological systems that provide many benefits to society. Throughout the western United States, these areas are valued as a source of water, recreational activities, and the unique plant and wildlife resources they support. Due to these myriad values, they also are among the most highly modified systems. Usually a single stream is owned and managed by multiple entities for purposes that often conflict to some extent. Thus, the ability to successfully manage a reach for a specific outcome is often influenced by uses both upstream and downstream of the site.

Although the above description is generic and applies to many streams, it aptly describes the portions of the North Fork Solomon River and Bow Creek managed by FWS. The values of this community are still apparent based on available data. However, past alterations both upstream and downstream of the refuge have caused significant changes that affect the ability of FWS to maintain the functions and processes that supported the historic riparian community. Of primary concern are the hydrologic alterations that result in extreme water level fluctuations in the floodplain. High water similar to that experienced in the mid-1990's may occur infrequently, but the cost of restoring the native community following such events likely will be time-consuming and costly. Further, this effort may be required every 20-30 years based on long-term predictions. Potential solutions that address the entire riparian community are not readily apparent because release of water from the reservoir during high flow periods would be required. This is not likely since a primary reason for reservoir construction was to store this water for irrigation below Kirwin. If a viable solution is not found, it is recommended that the benefits and costs associated with managing different portions of the riparian community be evaluated. This may result in the identification of portions that are relatively free of reservoir impacts. Part of this analysis would require determining the likelihood that certain reservoir elevations will occur during a given time period and estimating the riparian area impacted at these elevations. For example, a reservoir elevation of 528.8 m (1735.0 ft) would likely occur 2 times every 20 years. At this elevation, 20% of the riparian community would be flooded to depths that cause significant damage. Based on these probabilities, the riparian community could be divided into areas that are frequently and infrequently prone to reservoir impacts. Each of these areas could be addressed differently. For example, the area not prone to reservoir impacts could be managed to provide the full range of floristic composition and structure desired with a high level of probability that progress would not be impacted by the reservoir. In contrast, management effort in the area frequently experiencing reservoir impacts would differ because the benefits would be short-term and the cost excessive. This does not mean that this portion of the riparian community would be abandoned; rather a different set of management goals would be developed that take into account uncontrollable factors.

Upland
Kirwin NWR is within the central dissected, or mixed-grass, prairie region that historically was dominated by the bluestem-grama association (Launchbaugh and Owensby 1978). This association was prevalent on uplands in west-central Kansas, but also extended west on breaks into the dissected parts of the High Plains where the grama-buffalo grass prairie dominated the landscape. According to Kuchler (1974), the bluestem-grama association is characterized by dense communities of grasses and forbs that often are in two distinct layers: one of low-growing grasses and one of medium tall grasses and forbs that is usually more open. Dominant species are big and little bluestem, sideoats grama, and blue grama. Other characteristic species include western wheatgrass, western ragweed, leadplant, purple threeawn, hairy grama, buffalo grass, Freemont's clematis, purple coneflower, and Canada wildrye among others.

Factors historically controlling the distribution and physiognomy of the mixed-grass prairie included precipitation, fire, and herbivory. The plant species composing this prairie are sensitive to major precipitation fluctuations; thus, their distribution tends to move east and west in response to alternating periods of intense drought or wetness (Kuchler 1967,

1972). Summer fires (Sauer 1950) and herbivory (Dyksterhuis 1958) also helped maintain the prairie by suppressing woody vegetation. However, certain woody plants were always present as natural components in some areas (Kuchler 1974). Herbivores, including bison and smaller vertebrates such as prairie dogs, altered soil characteristics and other factors that influenced plant establishment and growth (Kuchler 1974).

Following the onset of human settlement, however, processes were modified that profoundly affected the prairie (Knopf and Samson 1997). Fire suppression, development and expansion of agricultural crops, changes in herbivores and herbivory, and planting of trees have significantly altered the prairie landscape. In addition, technological advances brought about other less obvious but equally important changes, including the development and introduction of new grasses and crops, groundwater pumping, herbicides, and fertilization. These and other actions have resulted in significant loss and fragmentation of the prairie community. For example, currently about 60% of Kansas lands are used for agriculture. Of this 60%, about 48% is cropland and the other 12% is non-native grasses (e.g., brome) or CRP (seeded natives).

The condition on Kirwin NWR is representative of the conditions for Kansas as a whole. The refuge encompasses about 2,833 ha (7,000 ac) of uplands at conservation pool and 2,712 ha (6,700 ac) at a pool elevation of 527.7 m (1,731.3 ft). Grasslands dominate this acreage, but the refuge staff reports that only about 81 ha (200 ac) of native grass occur on the refuge. The remainder is either pasture or reseeded grass. Further, much of the native grass is isolated (i.e., fragmented) and occurs in small blocks. Other habitats occurring in the uplands include shelterbelts, croplands, chalk bluffs, and a few temporary wetlands. Although the exact area of shelterbelts is not known, many appear to be 15-31 m (50-100 ft) wide and extend for various distances along roads and fence lines. The tree composition includes a mix of both hardwood and evergreen species. Wheat, sorghum, corn, and alfalfa are the dominant crops on the refuge and approximately 486 ha (1,200 ac) are planted annually when the reservoir is at an elevation of 527.1 m (1729.25 ft). The cropping program is designed to prepare agricultural land for conversion to grass and provide foods for migratory birds and resident wildlife. Farming is accomplished using cooperative farmers and arrangements vary depending on crop (refuge staff). For example, the refuge share of row crops is 25%, whereas stubble constitutes the refuge share of wheat.

Chalk outcroppings occur at higher elevations in the uplands, whereas only a few palustrine wetlands occur in depressional areas. Both of these communities exist as small, disjunct areas that compose only a small percentage of refuge lands. Although not covered in this report due to lack of information, both support some distinctive plant species and constitute unique habitats on the refuge. Thus, additional information should be obtained regarding their locations, sizes, and unique resources.

Most of the remaining discussion uses the grassland component of the uplands as the baseline condition. This approach was used because comparing and contrasting the values and management options of multiple plant communities without a standard for comparison is confusing. Grassland was selected as the standard because it represents the historic plant community and presently dominates the uplands. Also, the values and methods of managing other habitats (e.g., corn, shelterbelts) in the uplands are largely known and require little discussion.

Although much of the historic prairie on the refuge was converted or degraded prior to establishment, this community (excluding areas adjacent to the reservoir) appears to be the least effected by the reservoir. Consequently, FWS has more direct control and can likely influence future conditions more reliably. In general, the current condition of refuge grasslands varies greatly. There are small areas, many on the south side of the reservoir, that contain a high proportion of native grass and forb species. In contrast, other areas are primarily composed of non-native, cool season grasses. The dominant non-native species is smooth brome, but small areas of Kentucky bluegrass also are present (refuge staff). Finally, areas in various stages of restoration also occur on the refuge. Species composition of these stands is mixed, with the presence of both warm season natives and cool season non-natives. Unfortunately, more detailed information on the current condition of the grasslands is lacking. Maps depicting the locations and sizes of different grassland types (native, reseeded, tame) are not available, and both qualitative and quantitative information regarding the floristic composition (species of grasses, forbs) and structure of each type are unknown. Although all information is rarely available, the lack of at least some of the above information renders any comments incomplete and speculative. Therefore, the following information is provided as a recommendation regarding the types of information that should be developed prior to CCP development. In addition, examples are provided regarding potential uses of this information for developing future management direction.

First, the locations and floristic composition of the different grassland types should be determined. The most proficient method would be to develop a digital vegetation map based on floristics rather than generic terms such as pasture, reseeded grass, or native grass. The latter terms can be misleading if labels are not applied based on floristic attributes and often do not convey sufficient information to determine current value or management options. For example, the designation of native grass on the refuge appears to be based on the premise that the ground has never been plowed (e.g., unbroken sod is another frequently used term). Such a designation may be correct and provide some information, but definitions based solely on past management actions (or lack thereof) do not guarantee that floristic composition and/or structure are representative of the historic native community. For example, invasive grasses (e.g., smooth brome) can invade areas never plowed and alter plant and bird

community composition and structure (Wilson and Belcher 1989). Therefore, there is also no guarantee that the plant community will provide suitable habitat for vertebrates (e.g., birds) and invertebrates (e.g., butterflies) that are an important part of the grassland community.

Second, the current value of the different grassland communities identified during vegetation mapping must be determined. Many vertebrates and invertebrates exhibit plasticity and can tolerate certain changes in plant composition and/or structure. Thus, certain non-native communities, or mixed native/non-native communities, may provide sufficient value to warrant maintaining on the refuge. For example, row crops and wheat provide foods for select species of waterfowl, shelterbelts provide suitable habitat for certain songbirds, and CRP plantings that often include some non-native species provide benefits to some grassland birds. The benefits provided by these habitats must be compared to the potential benefits that would result from converting portions of these areas to other types. For example, shelterbelts provide habitat for some songbirds, but represent "hostile environments" that can hinder breeding by some grassland bird species. Thus, removing shelterbelts to increase the contiguous area of grasslands above a threshold size may benefit grassland birds but negatively impact songbird numbers. Such tradeoffs should be documented prior to making management decisions. Part of this analysis should also involve evaluating the spatial attributes (e.g., size, location) of each community. Appropriate floristic composition and structure is important, but many species also require areas of certain size, or multiple communities in close juxtaposition, to adequately meet life history requisites (Herkert 1994, Helzer and Jelinski 1999, Walk and Warner 1999). For example, some species of grassland birds known to occur on the refuge exhibit minimum area requirements for nesting. Therefore, the grassland areas that have been developed for public use may not constitute suitable habitat because the extensive road network may have fragmented these areas sufficiently, regardless of human activities associated with these areas.

Although a large amount of information exists on species-habitat relationships, attempts often are made to assess values based on opinions and past experiences. This often results in confusion and conflict. Therefore, it is recommended that objective information be developed prior to discussing the relative merits of each community. This may seem daunting, but much of the information on bird-habitat relationships has already been compiled for many species known to occur on the refuge, and additional research could be conducted. The digital vegetation map also would prove invaluable because it could be used to assess size of each community or distances between communities.

Third, the benefits and detriments of altering the type, size, or spatial location of various communities should be evaluated. For example, the removal of shelterbelts and/or cropland in certain areas may not result in the creation of contiguous grassland that exceeds a threshold required to meet the needs of certain avian species. In such cases, the costs of conversion would not be warranted because it would not result in expected benefits. Similarly, the public use facilities may fragment grasslands in the eastern portion of the refuge sufficiently to preclude nesting by some wildlife. If this were true, the benefits of managing these areas to provide specific structural conditions may not be worth the cost. If a digital vegetation map were available, various scenarios could be portrayed graphically to determine the best configuration and size of different community types.

Finally, information should be developed to evaluate the potential of accomplishing different activities. For example, statements made by the refuge staff suggest that the current conditions of most existing grasslands are not desirable. If an evaluation confirms this statement, then decisions must be made regarding the potential for different grassland areas. An initial step could involve classifying each grassland tract as being in need of either restoration or maintenance. This is an important distinction because maintenance implies that the existing floristic composition is acceptable and management is directed toward altering structural components (e.g., litter depth, height, density). Although not everything is known, the use of tools (fire, herbivory, mowing) to maintain grasslands has received considerable attention by the scientific community and general concepts exist regarding appropriate techniques. In contrast, true "prairie" restoration is much more difficult. A review of the literature suggests some techniques have reliably proven successful in establishing some components of prairie (e.g., warm season grass), but much remains to be learned regarding restoration of all components (e.g., forbs, native cool season grasses). This is particularly true of mixed-grass prairie. Little definitive information exists that provides guidance in determining appropriate site preparation, seed mixtures, or time and rate of seeding for different components relative to specific site conditions (e.g., soil type, groundwater table).

The lack of information for the existing grassland communities, in combination with the lack of proven restoration techniques for mixed-grass prairie, suggests that attempts to convert existing upland communities to native prairie will be difficult. However, this does not mean that an attempt should not be made. Rather, it indicates that success will require much work over numerous years (Kindscher and Tieszen 1998, Fuhlendorf et al. 2002), development of appropriate monitoring techniques, and frequent experimentation. An extensive search of the literature and consultations with local experts likely will provide initial guidance useful for identifying potential attributes that may influence restoration potential. This information could then be used to refine additional searches for refuge-specific information on these attributes. For example, if depths to groundwater or certain soil characteristics are deemed important, this information could be obtained from various sources and evaluated to determine the most likely locations to attempt restoration.

Management Potential – In many respects, FWS can exert the greatest influence on the upland community compared to other community types. However, constraints still exist that will influence future conditions. Uplands adjacent to the reservoir are wetter during high water years and extensive groundwater pumping upstream of the refuge likely has altered the subsurface hydrology of some upland habitats. The effects of these alterations are unknown, but research indicates change in the water table can effectively alter environmental conditions and, therefore, plant species occurrence (Currier 1988). Thus, literature reviews should be conducted to determine potential changes in abiotic conditions that would preclude certain management options. For example, restoration of native grasses and forbs adjacent to the reservoir may not be feasible due to changes in soil characteristics. If this is the case, another grassland type or habitat should be considered. In addition, invasive species have altered floristic and structural attributes of many grassland tracts. Although techniques have been developed for controlling many of these species, desirable vegetation must be established following control or there are no long-term biological benefits. The ability to accomplish this task largely will depend on what is considered a desirable community. Depending on the types of natural resource benefits the core team decides the refuge should provide, grasslands ranging from native mixed-grass prairie to CRP or tame grasses may be appropriate. Some of these types can be developed with a high degree of certainty, whereas others are very difficult to establish and maintain. Finally, some plant communities (e.g., shelterbelts, croplands) and the public use facilities were not present historically. Although such features may be considered obstructions from the perspective of historic conditions, they provide values that cannot, and should not, be ignored. Therefore, decisions must be made regarding the appropriate mix of historic and current conditions. These decisions will likely influence the types and configuration of the different communities composing the uplands.

Public Use

In addition to wildlife benefits, the refuge provides various forms of public recreation that should be mentioned. At conservation pool there are 1,402 ha (3,465 ac) of surface water (68.4% of reservoir) open to activities such as boat fishing, water skiing and jet skiing. In addition, about 41 ha (100 ac) of grassland adjacent to the main body of the reservoir are developed for public use, including shore fishing, camping, and picnicking (U. S. Bureau of Reclamation, URL http://www.usbr.gov/gp). There is also an extensive road network, including a tour loop around the perimeter of the refuge. Finally, hunting (deer and waterfowl primarily) is allowed in both the riparian and upland communities. Given the number and types of recreational visits to the refuge (U.S. Bureau of Reclamation 2002), it is possible that human activities could represent a disturbance that impacts some species that use the refuge. Peak waterfowl and shorebird migration periods do not appear to coincide with peak recreational periods (refuge staff). However, ground nesting ducks (e.g., Gadwall, Mallard), Least Terns, grassland birds, and species that nest in trees adjacent to deepwater habitat (e.g., Double-crested Cormorants, Great Blue Herons, and Bald Eagles) are present during the summer recreational period. Various regional and national plans consider populations of some of these species to be of concern (Appendix D) and information is available that indicates human activities can interfere with the successful rearing of young of these species. Despite these observations, which only allude to possibilities, there is not sufficient evidence to either confirm or discount conflicts. However, the fact that human-wildlife conflicts may occur identifies the need to develop specific information regarding potential detrimental impacts to wildlife. Scientific information addressing the effects of disturbance is available, but conditions on Kirwin NWR may differ from those reported elsewhere. Thus, definitive resolution of this concern may require conducting an appropriately designed monitoring program or research study on the refuge. Regardless of the source, this information could be used to develop solutions that eliminate or minimize impacts without negatively impacting public use opportunities.

Finally, the refuge staff has responsibility for enforcing regulations and maintaining facilities associated with recreational activities. Currently, the staff estimate that possibly 50 to 60% of their time is annually devoted to tasks associated with the public use program (refuge staff). This amount of effort, although often warranted, should be evaluated relative to the time required to achieve the biological goals established in the CCP. FWS should use this evaluation to determine an appropriate balance between natural resource and public use management, and adjust budgetary and time requirements to meet these needs.

Literature Cited

Albertson, F. W. 1937. Ecology of mixed prairie in west central Kansas. Ecological Monographs 7:481-547.

American Ornithologists' Union. 1998. Check-list of North American Birds. 7th edition. American Ornithologists' Union, Washington, D.C.

American Ornithologists' Union. 2000. Forty-second supplement to the American Ornithologists' Union Check-list of North American Birds. Auk 117:847-858.

American Ornithologists' Union. 2002. Forty-third supplement to the American Ornithologists' Union Check-list of North American Birds. Auk 119:897-906.

American Ornithologists' Union. 2003. Forty-fourth supplement to the American Ornithologists' Union Check-list of North American Birds. Auk 120:923-931.

Bailey, J. K., J. A. Schweitzer, and T. G. Whitman. 2001. Saltcedar negatively affects biodiversity of aquatic macroinvertebrates. Wetlands 21:442-447.

Baker, L. A. 1992. Introduction to nonpoint source pollution in the United States and prospects for wetland use. Ecological Engineering 1:1-26.

Callender, E., and J. A. Robbins. 1993. Transport and accumulation of radionuclides in stable elements in a Missouri River system. Water Resources Research 29:1787-1804.

Carothers, S. W., R. R. Johnson, and S. W Aitchison. 1974. Population structure and social organization of southwestern riparian birds. American Zoologist 14:97-108.

Christensen, V. G. 1999. Deposition of selenium and other constituents in reservoir bottom sediment of the Solomon River Basin, north-central Kansas. U.S. Geological Survey, Water Resources Investigations Report 99-4230.

Christensen, V. G., and K. E. Juracek. 2001. Variability of metals in reservoir sediment from two adjacent basins in the central Great Plains. Environmental Geology 40:470-481.

Currier, P. J. 1988. Plant species composition and groundwater levels in a Platte River wet meadow. Pages 19-24 *in* T. B. Bragg and J. Stubbendieck, editors. Proceedings of the 11th North American Prairie Conference. University of Nebraska, Lincoln, Nebraska.

Dieter, C. D. 1990. Causes and effects of water turbidity: a selected annotated bibliography. South Dakota Cooperative Wildlife Research Unit, South Dakota State University, Technical Bulletin Number 5.

Dyksterhuis, E. J. 1958. Range conservation as based on sites and conditions classes. Journal of Soil and Water Conservation 13:151-155.

Eddy, T. A. 1994. Phreatophyte survey and water-use estimates for nine river systems in Kansas. Proceedings of the 14th Annual North American Prairie Conference. Kansas State University, Manhattan, Kansas.

Fellows, S., K. Stone, S. L. Jones, N. Damude, and S. Brown. 2001. Central plains / playa lakes regional shorebird conservation plan. Version 1. URL: http://shorebirdplan.fws.gov/RegionalShorebird/RegionalPlans.htm

Fleharty, E. D. 1995. Wild animals and settlers on the Great Plains. University of Oklahoma Press, Norman.

Forman, R. T. T. 1995. Land mosaics: the ecology of landscapes and regions. Cambridge University Press, New York, New York.

Fredrickson, L. H. 1991. Strategies for water level manipulations in moist-soil systems. U. S. Fish and Wildlife Service, Waterfowl Management Handbook, Fish and Wildlife Leaflet 13.4.6.

Fredrickson, L. H., and M. K. Laubhan. 1994. Managing wetlands for wildlife. Pages 623-647 *in* T. A. Bookhout, editor. Research and management techniques for wildlife and habitats. Fifth edition. The Wildlife Society, Besthesda, Maryland.

Fredrickson, L. H., and F. A. Reid. 1986. Wetland and riparian habitats: a nongame overview. Pages 58-96 in J. B. Hale, L. B. Best, and R. L. Clawson, editors. Management of nongame wildlife in the midwest: a developing art. North-Central Section, The Wildlife Society, Grand Rapids, Michigan.

Fuhlendorf, S. D., H. Zhang, T. R. Tunnell, D. M. Engle, and A. F. Cross. 2002. Effects of grazing on restoration of southern mixed prairie soils. Restoration Ecology 10:401-407

Gawlik, D. E. 2002. The effects of prey availability on the numerical response of wading birds. Ecological Monograph 72:329-346.

Helzer, C. J. and D. E. Jelinski. 1999. The relative importance of patch area and perimeter-area ratio to grassland breeding birds. Ecological Applications 9:1448-1458.

Herkert, J. R. 1994. The effects of habitat fragmentation on Midwestern grassland bird communities. Ecological Applications 4:461-471.

Hem, J. D. 1992. Study and interpretation of the chemical characteristics of natural water. Third edition. U. S. Geological Survey Water-Supply Paper 2254.

Igl, L. D. 1996. Bird checklists of the United States. Jamestown, ND. Northern Prairie Wildlife Research Center Home Page. http://www.npwrc.usgs.gov/resource/othrdata/chekbird/chekbird.htm (Version 12MAY03).

Johnson, W. C., and A. F. Arbogast. 1993. Geologic map, Phillips County. Kansas Geological Survey, Map M-29.

Kindscher, K., and L. L. Tieszen. 1998. Floristic and soil organic changes after fire and thirty-five years of native tallgrass prairie restoration. Restoration Ecology 5:181-196.

Knopf, F. L., and F. B. Samson. 1997. Conservation of grassland vertebrates. Ecological Studies 125:273-289.

Krull, J. N. 1970. Aquatic plant-macroinvertebrate associations and waterfowl. Journal of Wildlife Management 34:707-718.

Kuchler, A. W. 1967. Some geographic features of the Kansas prairie. Transactions of the Kansas Academy of Science 70:388-401.

Kuchler, A. W. 1972. The oscillations of the mixed prairie in Kansas. Erdkunde 26:120-129.

Kuchler, A. W. 1974. A new vegetation map of Kansas. Ecology 55:586-604.

Kullberg, R. G. 1974. Distribution of aquatic macrophytes related to paper mill effluents in a southern Michigan stream. American Midland Naturalist 91:271-281.

Kushlan, J. A., M. J. Steinkamp, K. C. Parsons, J. Capp, M. A. Cruz, M. Coulter, I. Davidson, L. Dickson, N. Edelson, R. Elliot, R. M. Erwin, S. Hatch S. Kress, R. Milko, S. Miller, K. Mills, R. Paul, R. Phillips, J. E. Saliva, B. Sydeman, J. Trapp, J. Wheeler, and K. Wohl. 2002. Waterbird Conservation for the Americas: The North American Waterbird Conservation Plan, version 1. Waterbird Conservation for the Americas, Washington, D.C.

Launchbaugh, J. L., and C. E. Owensby. 1978. Kansas rangelands: their management based on a half century of research. Kansas Agricultural Experiment Station Bulletin 622.

Leck, M. A. 1989. Wetland seed banks. Pages 283-305 in M. A. Leck, V. T. Parker, and R. L. Simpson, editors. Ecology of soil seed banks. Academic Press, San Diego, California.

Lemly, D. A., and G. J. Smith. 1987. Aquatic cycling of selenium – implications for fish and wildlife. U. S. Fish and Wildlife Service, Fish and Wildlife Leaflet 12.

Leonard, A. R. 1952. Geology and ground-water resources of the North Fork Solomon River in Mitchell, Osborne, Smith, and Phillips counties, Kansas. State Geological Survey of Kansas. Bulletin 98.

Mitsch, W. J., and J. G. Gosselink. 1993. Wetlands. Second edition. Van Nostrand Reinhold, New York, New York.

Moore, R. C., and K. K. Landes. 1937. Geologic map of Kansas. Kansas Geological Survey.

Pais, I., and J. B. Jones, Jr. 1997. The handbook of trace elements. St. Lucie Press, Boca Raton, Florida.

Palmer, W. C, 1965: Meteorological drought. Research Paper Number 45. Department of Commerce, Washington, D.C.

Pashley, D. N., C. J. Beardmore, J. A. Fitzgerald, R. P. Ford, W. C. Hunter, M. S. Morrison, and K. V. Rosenberg. 2000. Partners In Flight: Conservation of the land birds of the United States. American Bird Conservancy, The Plains, Virginia.

Phillips, M. A. 1980. Ground-Water Reconnaissance of the North Fork Solomon River Basin above Kirwin Dam Northwest Kansas. U. S. Bureau of Reclamation, Water and Power Resources Service, Region 7, Denver, Colorado.

Rezsutek, M. J. 1990. Associations of small mammals of Kirwin National Wildlife Refuge. Masters Thesis, Fort Hays State University, Fort Hays, Kansas.

Rich, T. D., C. J. Beardmore, H. Berlanga, P. J. Blancher, M. S. W. Bradstreet, G. S. Butcher, D. W. Demarest, E. H. Dunn, W. C. Hunter, E. E. Iñigo-Elias, J. A. Kennedy, A. M. Martell, A. O. Panjabi, D. N. Pashley, K. V. Rosenberg, C. M. Rustay, J. S. Wendt, T. C. Will. 2004. Partners in Flight North American Landbird Conservation Plan. Cornell Lab of Ornithology, Ithaca, New York.

Ritchie, J.C., C. M. Cooper, and J. R. McHenry. 1986. Sediment accumulation rates in lakes and reservoirs in the Mississippi River Valley. Pages 1357-1365 *in* S. Y. Wang, H. W. Shen, and L.Z. Ding, editors. River Sedimentation. University of Mississippi Press, Oxford.

Robel, R. J. 1961. Water depth and turbidity in relation to growth of sago pondweed. Journal of Wildlife Management 25:436-438.

Ross, J. A., compiler. 1991. Geologic map of Kansas. Kansas Geologic Survey, Map M-23, 1:500,000.

Saab, V. 1999. Importance of spatial scale to habitat use by breeding birds in riparian forests: a hierarchical analysis. Ecological Applications 9:135-151.

Sauer, C. O. 1950. Grassland climax, fire, and man. Journal of Range Management 3:16-21.

Sauer, J. R., J. E. Hines, and J. Fallon. 2004. The North American Breeding Bird Survey, Results and Analysis 1966 - 2003. USGS Patuxent Wildlife Research Center, Laurel, Maryland Version 2004.1. Available online at URL http://www.mbr-pwrc.usgs.gov/bbs/bbs.html.

Scott, M. L., M. A. Wondzell, and G. T. Auble. 1993. Hydrograph characteristics relevant to the establishment and growth of western riparian vegetation. Pages 237-246 *in* H. J. Morel-Seytoux, editor. Proceedings of the thirteenth annual American Geophysical Union Hydrology Days. Hydrology Days Publications, Atherton, California.

Sevigny, M. S. 1998. Foraging behavior and habitat selection by spring migrants in north central Kansas. Ms. Thesis, Fort Hays State University, Fort Hays, Kansas.

Skagen, S. K., and F. L. Knopf. 1994. Migrating shorebirds and habitat dynamics at a prairie wetland complex. Wilson Bulletin 106:91-105.

Sudbrock, A. 1993. Tamarisk control. I. Fighting back: an overview of the invasion, and a low-impact way of fighting it. Restoration Management Notes 11:31-34.

Teskey, R. D., and T. M. Hinckley. 1977. Impact of water level changes on woody riparian and wetland communities, Volume I: Plant and soil resources. U. S. Fish and Wildlife Service, Biological Services Program. FWS/OBS-77/58.

Urban, D. L., and T. M. Smith. 1989. Microhabitat pattern and the structure of forest bird communities. American Naturalist 133:811-829.

U. S. Bureau of Reclamation. 1984. Solomon River Basin water management study, Kansas. U. S. Department of the Interior, Special Report.

U. S. Bureau of Reclamation. 2002. Solomon River Basin final environmental assessment: conversion of long-term water service contracts to repayment contracts. Nebraska-Kansas Area Office, Grand Island, Nebraska.

U. S. Fish and Wildlife Service. 1996. Kirwin National Wildlife Refuge Comprehensive Management Plan. Denver, Colorado.

U. S. Fish and Wildlife Service. 2002. Birds of conservation concern 2002. Division of Migratory Bird Management, Arlington, Virginia. 99 pp. Online version available at http://migratorybirds.fws.gov/reports/ bcc2002.pdf.

van der Valk, A. G., and C. B. Davis. 1978. The role of seed-banks in the vegetation dynamics of prairie glacial marshes. Ecology 59:322-335.

Voigts, D. K. 1976. Aquatic invertebrate abundance in relation to changing marsh vegetation. American Midland Naturalist 95:313-322.

Walk, J. W., and R. E. Warner. 1999. Effects of habitat area on the occurrence of grassland birds in Illinois. American Midland Naturalist 141:339-344.

Wiens, J. A. 1989. Spatial scaling in ecology. Functional Ecology 3:385-387.

Wilson, S. D., and J. W. Belcher. 1989. Plant and bird communities of native prairie and introduced Eurasian vegetation in Manitoba, Canada. Conservation Biology 3:39-44.

Appendix A.

Potential information needs that may be required to address the recommendations provided in the evaluation section.

Potential information needs	Deepwater	Shoreline	Riparian	Upland
Abiotic				
Bathymetry data			X	X
Hydrology				
Groundwater			X	X
Reservoir pool elevations	X	X	X	X
River hydrographs			X	
Literature synthesis on processes			X	X
Monitoring protocols and methods	X	X	X	X
Soils (digital map and base data)	X	X	X	X
Water quality criteria for aquatic plants	X	X		
Vegetation				
Composition/structure	X	X	X	X
Digital map based on floristics			X	X
Maintenance techniques			X	X
Monitoring protocols and methods	X	X	X	X
Plant germination/growth requirements	X	X	X	X
Restoration techniques			X	X
Wildlife				
Abundance data	X	X	X	X
Activity data	X	X	X	X
Monitoring protocols and methods	X	X	X	X
Species-habitat relationships	X	X	X	X
Digital orthophoto quads (multiple years)	X	X	X	X
Annual changes in fish biomass	X			
Area of closed zone and crops	X			X
Cost (time/money) of managing public use facilities	X	X		X
Cost of biological activities		X	X	X

Appendix B.

Scientific and common names of vertebrates and plants. Bold indicates species that have been recorded as nesting. Information on fish, amphibians, and reptiles obtained from Kansas Department of Wildlife and Parks (refuge files dated 01/30/2003).

Common Name	Scientific Name	Common Name	Scientific Name

Amphibians

Bullfrog	*Rana catesbeiana*		
Great plains narrowmouth frog	*Gastrophryne olivacea*		
Great plains toad	*Bufo cognatus*		
Northern cricket frog	*Acris crepitans*		
Plains leopard frog	*Rana blairi*		
Plains spadefoot	*Scaphiopus bombifrons*		
Rocky mountain toad	*Bufo woodhousii*		
Tiger salamander	*Ambystoma tigrinum*		

Birds

Common Name	Scientific Name	Common Name	Scientific Name
Greater White-fronted Goose	*Anser albifrons*	Cooper's Hawk	*Accipiter cooperii*
Snow Goose	*Chen caerulescens*	Northern Goshawk	*Accipiter gentilis*
Ross's Goose	*Chen rossii*	Red-shouldered Hawk	*Buteo lineatus*
Canada Goose	***Branta canadensis***	**Swainson's Hawk**	***Buteo swainsoni***
Trumpeter Swan	*Cygnus buccinator*	**Red-tailed Hawk**	***Buteo jamaicensis***
Tundra Swan	*Cygnus columbianus*	Ferruginous Hawk	*Buteo regalis*
Wood Duck	***Aix sponsa***	Rough-legged Hawk	*Buteo lagopus*
Gadwall	***Anas strepera***	Golden Eagle	*Aquila chrysaetos*
American Wigeon	*Anas americana*	American Kestrel	*Falco sparverius*
American Black Duck	*Anas rubripes*	Merlin	*Falco columbarius*
Mallard	***Anas platyrhynchos***	Peregrine Falcon	*Falco peregrinus*
Blue-winged Teal	***Anas discors***	Prairie Falcon	*Falco mexicanus*
Cinnamon Teal	*Anas cyanoptera*	Virginia Rail	*Rallus limicola*
Northern Shoveler	***Anas clypeata***	Sora	*Porzana carolina*
Northern Pintail	***Anas acuta***	American Coot	*Fulica americana*
Green-winged Teal	***Anas crecca***	Sandhill Crane	*Grus canadensis*
Canvasback	*Aythya valisineria*	Whooping Crane	*Grus americana*
Redhead	*Aythya americana*	Black-bellied Plover	*Pluvialis squatarola*
Ring-necked Duck	*Aythya collaris*	American Golden-Plover	*Pluvialis dominica*
Greater Scaup	*Aythya marila*	Snowy Plover	*Charadrius alexandrinus*
Lesser Scaup	*Aythya affinis*	Semipalmated Plover	*Charadrius semipalmatus*
Bufflehead	*Bucephala albeola*	Piping Plover	*Charadrius melodus*
Common Goldeneye	*Bucephala clangula*	Killdeer	*Charadrius vociferus*
Hooded Merganser	*Lophodytes cucullatus*	Black-necked Stilt	*Himantopus mexicanus*
Common Merganser	*Mergus merganser*	American Avocet	*Recurvirostra americana*
Ruddy Duck	*Oxyura jamaicensis*	Greater Yellowlegs	*Tringa melanoleuca*
Ring-necked Pheasant	***Phasianus colchicus***	Lesser Yellowlegs	*Tringa flavipes*
Greater Prairie-Chicken	*Tympanuchus cupido*	Willet	*Catoptrophorus semipalmatus*
Wild Turkey	*Meleagris gallopavo*	Spotted Sandpiper	*Actitis macularia*
Northern Bobwhite	***Colinus virginianus***	Upland Sandpiper	*Bartramia longicauda*
Common Loon	*Gavia immer*	Long-billed Curlew	*Numenius americanus*
Pied-billed Grebe	*Podilymbus podiceps*	Hudsonian Godwit	*Limosa haemastica*
Horned Grebe	*Podiceps auritus*	Marbled Godwit	*Limosa fedoa*
Eared Grebe	*Podiceps nigricollis*	Ruddy Turnstone	*Arenaria interpres*
Western Grebe	*Aechmophorus occidentalis*	Sanderling	*Calidris alba*
American White Pelican	*Pelecanus erythrorhynchos*	Semipalmated Sandpiper	*Calidris pusilla*
Double-crested Cormorant	***Phalacrocorax auritus***	Western Sandpiper	*Calidris mauri*
American Bittern	*Botaurus lentiginosus*	Least Sandpiper	*Calidris minutilla*
Least Bittern	*Ixobrychus exilis*	White-rumped Sandpiper	*Calidris fuscicollis*
Great Blue Heron	*Ardea herodias*	Baird's Sandpiper	*Calidris bairdii*
Great Egret	*Ardea alba*	Dunlin	*Calidris alpina*
Snowy Egret	*Egretta thula*	Stilt Sandpiper	*Calidris himantopus*
Little Blue Heron	*Egretta caerulea*	Buff-breasted Sandpiper	*Tryngites subruficollis*
Cattle Egret	*Bubulcus ibis*	Long-billed Dowitcher	*Limnodromus scolopaceus*
Green Heron	*Butorides virescens*	Common Snipe	*Gallinago gallinago*
Black-crowned Night-Heron	*Nycticorax nycticorax*	Wilson's Phalarope	*Phalaropus tricolor*
Yellow-crowned Night-Heron	*Nyctanassa violacea*	Franklin's Gull	*Larus pipixcan*
White-faced Ibis	*Plegadis chihi*	Bonaparte's Gull	*Larus philadelphia*
Turkey Vulture	*Cathartes aura*	Ring-billed Gull	*Larus delawarensis*
Osprey	*Pandion haliaetus*	Herring Gull	*Larus argentatus*
Mississippi Kite	*Ictinia mississippiensis*	Glaucous Gull	*Larus hyperboreus*
Bald Eagle	*Haliaeetus leucocephalus*	Caspian Tern	*Sterna caspia*
Northern Harrier	*Circus cyaneus*	Common Tern	*Sterna hirundo*
Sharp-shinned Hawk	*Accipiter striatus*	Forster's Tern	*Sterna forsteri*
		Least Tern	***Sterna antillarum***
		Black Tern	*Chlidonias niger*
		Rock Pigeon	*Columba livia*
		Mourning Dove	***Zenaida macroura***
		Black-billed Cuckoo	***Coccyzus erythrophthalmus***
		Yellow-billed Cuckoo	***Coccyzus americanus***
		Barn Owl	***Tyto alba***
		Eastern Screech-Owl	***Megascops asio***
		Great Horned Owl	***Bubo virginianus***
		Snowy Owl	*Bubo scandiacus*
		Burrowing Owl	***Athene cunicularia***
		Barred Owl	*Strix varia*

Common Name	Scientific Name	Common Name	Scientific Name
Short-eared Owl	*Asio flammeus*	Yellow-breasted Chat	*Icteria virens*
Common Nighthawk	***Chordeiles minor***	Spotted Towhee	*Pipilo maculatus*
Chimney Swift	*Chaetura pelagica*	Eastern Towhee	*Pipilo erythrophthalmus*
Belted Kingfisher	*Ceryle alcyon*	American Tree Sparrow	*Spizella arborea*
Red-headed Woodpecker	***Melanerpes erythrocephalus***	Chipping Sparrow	*Spizella passerina*
Red-bellied Woodpecker	*Melanerpes carolinus*	Clay-colored Sparrow	*Spizella pallida*
Downy Woodpecker	***Picoides pubescens***	Brewer's Sparrow	*Spizella breweri*
Hairy Woodpecker	*Picoides villosus*	Field Sparrow	*Spizella pusilla*
Northern Flicker	*Colaptes auratus*	Vesper Sparrow	*Pooecetes gramineus*
Eastern Wood-Pewee	*Contopus virens*	**Lark Sparrow**	***Chondestes grammacus***
Willow flycatcher	*Empidonax traillii*	Lark Bunting	*Calamospiza melanocorys*
Least flycatcher	*Empidonax minimus*	Grasshopper Sparrow	*Ammodramus savannarum*
Eastern Phoebe	***Sayornis phoebe***	Baird's Sparrow	*Ammodramus bairdii*
Say's Phoebe	*Sayornis saya*	Henslow's Sparrow	*Ammodramus henslowii*
Great Crested Flycatcher	*Myiarchus crinitus*	Song Sparrow	*Melospiza melodia*
Western Kingbird	***Tyrannus verticalis***	Lincoln's Sparrow	*Melospiza lincolnii*
Eastern Kingbird	***Tyrannus tyrannus***	White-throated Sparrow	*Zonotrichia albicollis*
Scissor-tailed Flycatcher	*Tyrannus forficatus*	Harris's Sparrow	*Zonotrichia querula*
Loggerhead Shrike	***Lanius ludovicianus***	White-crowned Sparrow	*Zonotrichia leucophrys*
Bell's Vireo	*Vireo bellii*	Dark-eyed Junco	*Junco hyemalis*
Yellow-throated Vireo	*Vireo flavifrons*	Lapland Longspur	*Calcarius lapponicus*
Plumbeous Vireo	*Vireo plumbeus*	Chestnut-collared Longspur	*Calcarius ornatus*
Warbling Vireo	*Vireo gilvus*	**Northern Cardinal**	***Cardinalis cardinalis***
Red-eyed Vireo	*Vireo olivaceus*	Rose-breasted Grosbeak	*Pheucticus ludovicianus*
Blue Jay	***Cyanocitta cristata***	Black-headed Grosbeak	*Pheucticus melanocephalus*
Black-billed Magpie	***Pica hudsonia***	Blue Grosbeak	*Passerina caerulea*
American Crow	*Corvus brachyrhynchos*	Lazuli Bunting	*Passerina amoena*
Horned Lark	***Eremophila alpestris***	Indigo Bunting	*Passerina cyanea*
Purple Martin	*Progne subis*	**Dickcissel**	***Spiza americana***
Northern Rough-winged Swallow	*Stelgidopteryx serripennis*	Bobolink	*Dolichonyx oryzivorus*
Bank Swallow	*Riparia riparia*	Red-winged Blackbird	*Agelaius phoeniceus*
Cliff Swallow	*Petrochelidon pyrrhonota*	**Eastern Meadowlark**	***Sturnella magna***
Barn Swallow	***Hirundo rustica***	**Western Meadowlark**	***Sturnella neglecta***
Black-capped Chickadee	*Poecile atricapillus*	Yellow-headed Blackbird	*Xanthocephalus xanthocephalus*
Red-breasted Nuthatch	*Sitta canadensis*	Brewer's Blackbird	*Euphagus cyanocephalus*
White-breasted Nuthatch	*Sitta carolinensis*	Common Grackle	*Quiscalus quiscula*
Brown Creeper	*Certhia americana*	Brown-headed Cowbird	*Molothrus ater*
House Wren	***Troglodytes aedon***	**Orchard Oriole**	***Icterus spurius***
Winter Wren	*Troglodytes troglodytes*	Bullock's Oriole	*Icterus bullockii*
Golden-crowned Kinglet	*Regulus satrapa*	Baltimore Oriole	*Icterus galbula*
Ruby-crowned Kinglet	*Regulus calendula*	Scott's Oriole	*Icterus parisorum*
Eastern Bluebird	*Sialia sialis*	House Finch	*Carpodacus mexicanus*
Mountain Bluebird	*Sialia currucoides*	Common Redpoll	*Carduelis flammea*
Veery	*Catharus fuscescens*	Pine Siskin	*Carduelis pinus*
Swainson's Thrush	*Catharus ustulatus*	American Goldfinch	*Carduelis tristis*
Hermit Thrush	*Catharus guttatus*	House Sparrow	*Passer domesticus*
American Robin	***Turdus migratorius***		
Gray Catbird	*Dumetella carolinensis*		
Northern Mockingbird	***Mimus polyglottos***		

Fishes

Common Name	Scientific Name
Brown Thrasher	***Toxostoma rufum***
European Starling	***Sturnus vulgaris***
American Pipit	*Anthus rubescens*
Cedar Waxwing	*Bombycilla cedrorum*
Tennessee Warbler	*Vermivora peregrina*
Orange-crowned Warbler	*Vermivora celata*
Yellow Warbler	*Dendroica petechia*
Magnolia Warbler	*Dendroica magnolia*
Yellow-rumped Warbler	*Dendroica coronata*
Black-throated Gray Warbler	*Dendroica nigrescens*
Townsend's Warbler	*Dendroica townsendi*
Prairie Warbler	*Dendroica discolor*
Blackpoll Warbler	*Dendroica striata*
Black-and-white Warbler	*Mniotilta varia*
American Redstart	*Setophaga ruticilla*
Ovenbird	*Seiurus aurocapilla*
Northern Waterthrush	*Seiurus noveboracensis*
MacGillivray's Warbler	*Oporornis tolmiei*
Common Yellowthroat	*Geothlypis trichas*

Common Name	Scientific Name
Black bullhead	*Ictalurus melas*
Channel catfish	*Ictalurus punctatus*
Flathead catfish	*Pylodictis olivaris*
Black crappie	*Pomoxis nigromaculatus*
Bluegill	*Lepomis macrochirus*
Freshwater drum	*Aplodinotus grunniens*
Green sunfish	*Lepomis cyanellus*
Largemouth bass	*Micropterus salmoides*
Orangespotted sunfish	*Lepomis humilis*
Walleye	*Stizostedion vitreum*
White bass	*Morone chrysops*
White crappie	*Pomoxis annularis*
Wiper	*Morone chrysops* X *M. Saxatilis*
Common carp	*Cyprinus carpio*
Creek chub	*Semotilus atromaculatus*
Red shiner	*Cyprinella lutrensis*
River carpsucker	*Carpiodes carpio*
Sand shiner	*Notropis stramineus*

Common Name	Scientific Name	Common Name	Scientific Name
Gizzard shad	*Dorosoma cepedianum*	Siberian elm	*Ulmus pumila*
Plains killifish	*Fundulus zebrinu*	Willow	*Salix* spp.

Mammals

Bison	*Bison bison*
Prairie dog	*Cynomys* spp.

Plants

Beggarticks	*Bidens* spp.
Canada thistle	*Cirsium arvense*
Cocklebur	*Xanthium* sp.
Purple coneflower	*Echinacea purpurea*
Western ragweed	*Ambrosia psilostachya*
Smartweed	*Polygonum* spp.
Freemont's clematis	*Clematis fremontii*
cattail	*Typha* sp.
Big bluestem	*Andropogon gerardii*
Blue grama	*Bouteloua gracilis*
Bluestem	*Andropogon* spp.
Buffalo grass	*Buchloe dactyloides*
Bulrush	*Scirpus* spp.
Canada wildrye	*Elymus canadensis*
Corn	*Zea mays*
Hairy grama	*Bouteloua hirsuta*
Indiangrass	*Sorghastrum nutans*
Kentucky bluegrass	*Poa pratensis*
Little bluestem	*Schizachyrium scoparium*
Millet	*Echinochloa* spp.
Oats	*Avena* sp.
Panic grass	*Panicum* sp.
Prairie cordgrass	*Spartina pectinata*
Purple threeawn	*Aristida purpurea*
Reed canary grass	*Phalaris arundinacea*
Ricecut grass	*Leersia* sp.
Sedge	*Carex* spp.
Sideoats grama	*Bouteloua curtipendula*
Smooth brome	*Bromus inermis*
Sorghum	*Sorghum* sp.
Spikerush	*Eleocharis* spp.
Switchgrass	*Panicum virgatum*
Western wheatgrass	*Pascopyrum smithii*
Wheat	*Triticum* sp.
Meads milkweed	*Asclepias meadii*
Western prairie-fringed orchid	*Platanthera praeclara*
Alfalfa	*Medicago sativa*
Leadplant	*Amorpha canescens*
Soybean	*Glycine* sp.
Pondweed	*Potamogeton* spp.
American elm	*Ulmus americana*
Boxelder	*Acer negundo*
Cottonwood	*Populus* sp.
Eastern cottonwood	*Populus deltoides*
Green ash	*Fraxinus pennsylvanica*
Hackberry	*Celtis occidentalis*
Honey locust	*Gleditsia triacanthos*
Mulberry	*Morus* spp.
Peachleaved willow	*Salix amygdaloides*
Saltcedar	*Tamarix* sp.

Reptiles

Eastern fence lizard	*Sceloporus undulatus*
Five-lined skink	*Eumeces fasciatus*
Great plains skink	*Eumeces obsoletus*
Lesser earless lizard	*Holbrookia maculata*
Slender glass lizard	*Ophisaurus attenuatus*
Texas horned lizard	*Phrynosoma cornutum*
Brown snake	*Storeria dekayi*
Bull snake	*Pituophis melanoleucus*
Coachwhip	*Masticophis flagellum*
Common garter snake	*Thamnophis sirtalis*
Common kingsnake	*Lampropeltis getula*
Eastern hognose snake	*Heterodon platirhinos*
Lined snake	*Tropidoclonion lineatum*
Milk snake	*Lampropeltis triangulum*
Northern water snake	*Nerodia sipedon*
Plains blackhead snake	*Tantilla nigriceps*
Plains garter snake	*Thamnophis radix*
Prairie rattlesnake	*Crotalus viridis*
Rat snake	*Elaphe obsoleta*
Ringneck snake	*Diadophis punctatus*
Western hognose snake	*Heterodon nasicus*
Western ribbon snake	*Thamnophis proximus*
Yellow-bellied racer	*Coluber constrictor*

Turtles

Alligator snapping turtle	*Macroclemys temmincki*
Common snapping turtle	*Chelydra serpentine*
Ornate box turtle	*Terrapene ornata*
Smooth softshell turtle	*Apalone mutica*
Spiny softshell turtle	*Apalone spinifera*
Western painted turtle	*Chrysemys picta*
Yellow mud turtle	*Kinosternon flavescens*

Appendix C.

Total annual use days, average annual populations, and peak populations, respectively for the following waterfowl groups using Kirwin National Wildlife Refuge between 1983 and 2001: American Coot and dabbling ducks excluding Mallard (a – c), diving ducks (d – f), Canada Goose and Mallard (g – i), and White-fronted Goose and Snow Goose (j – k).

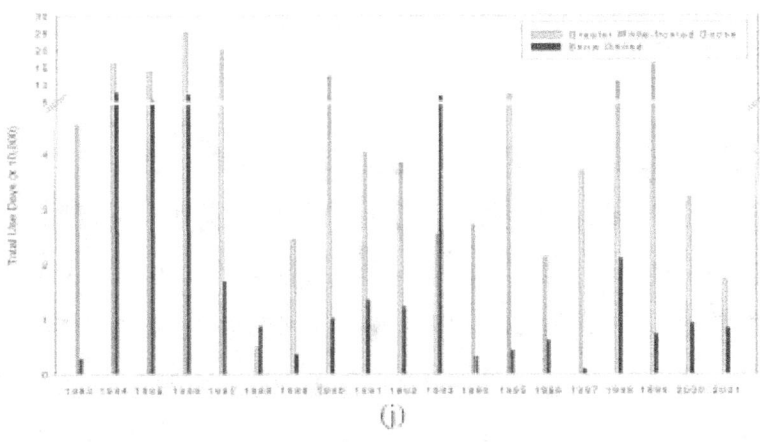

(j)

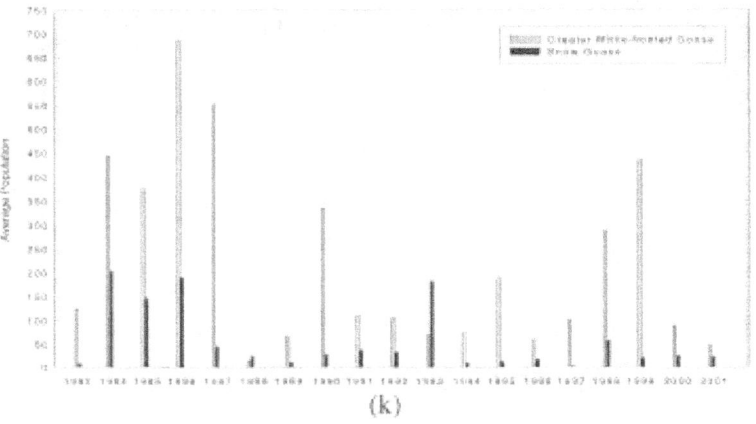

(k)

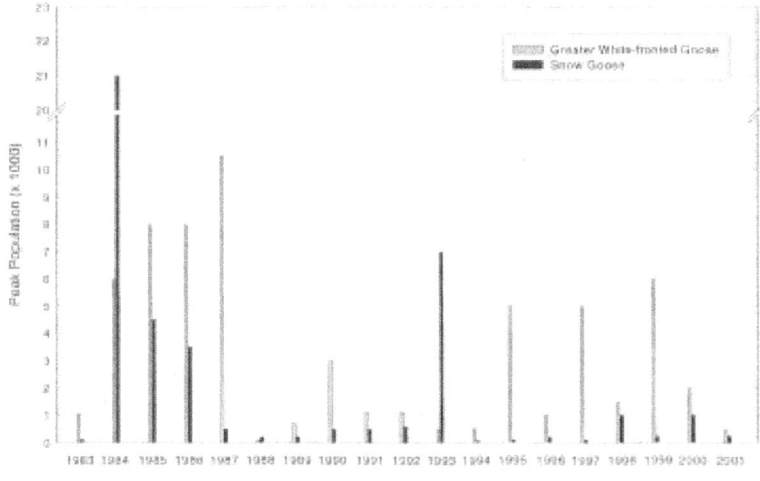

(l)

34

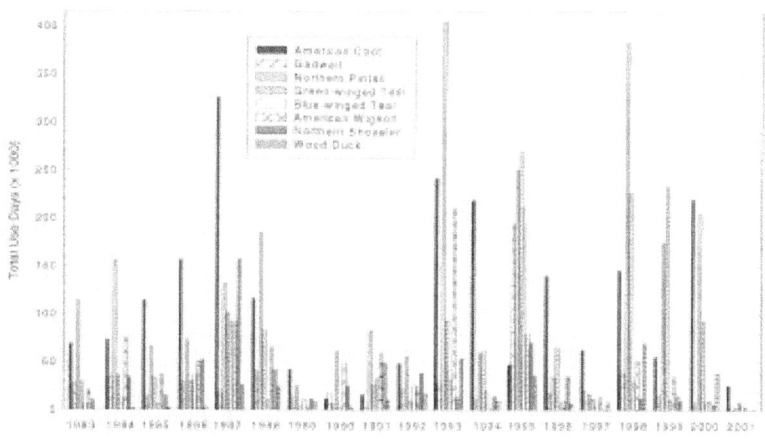

(a)

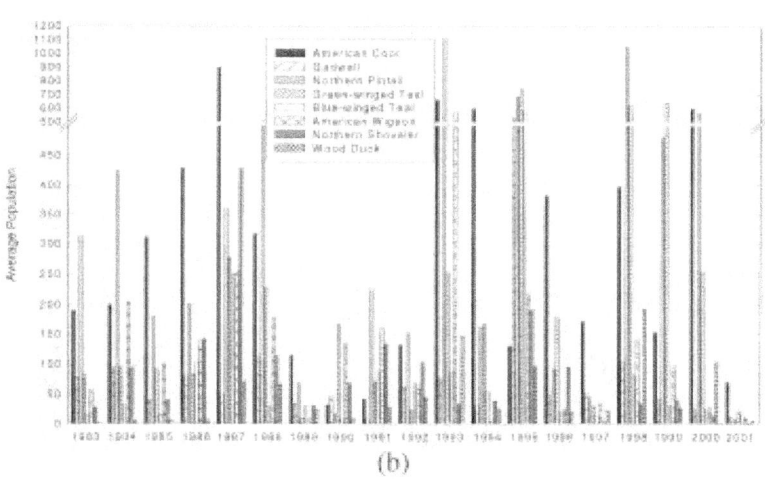

(b)

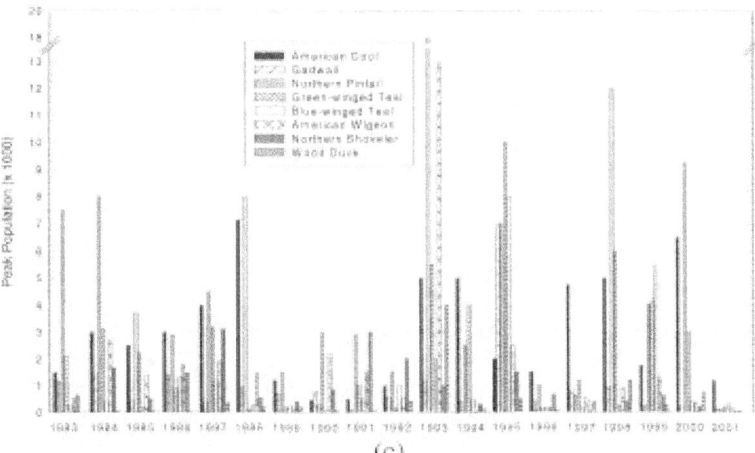

(c)

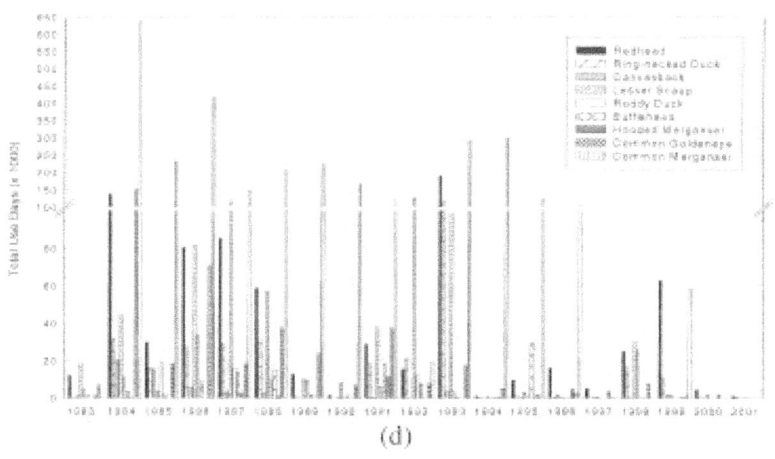

(d)

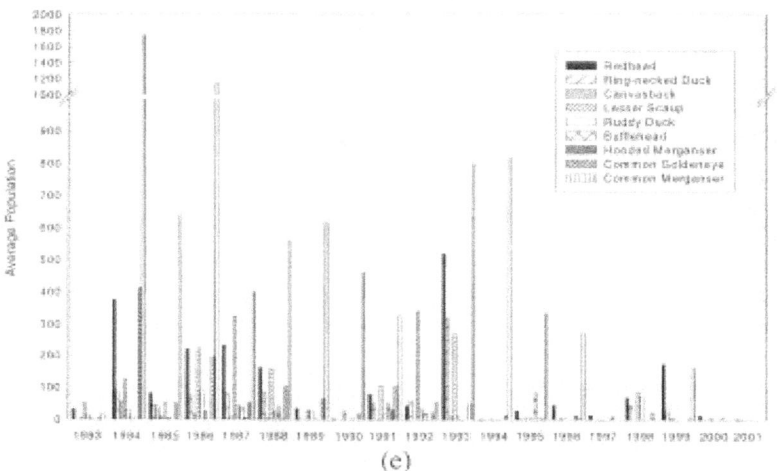

(e)

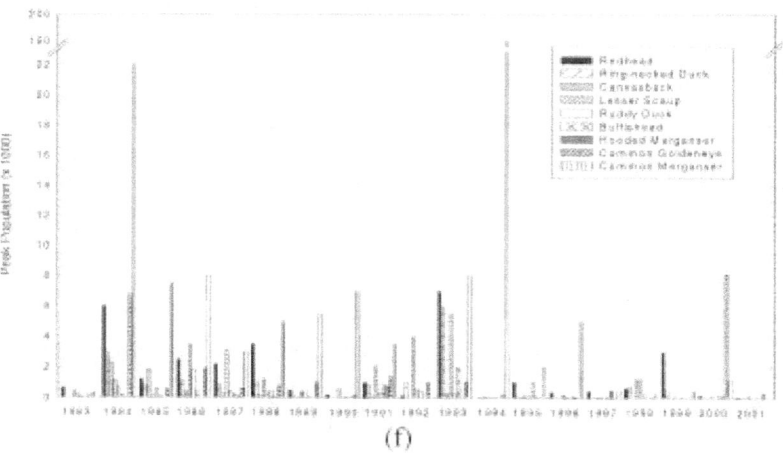

(f)

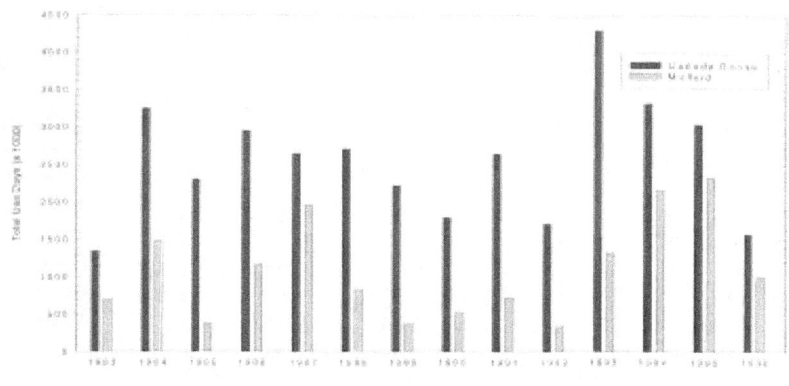

(g)

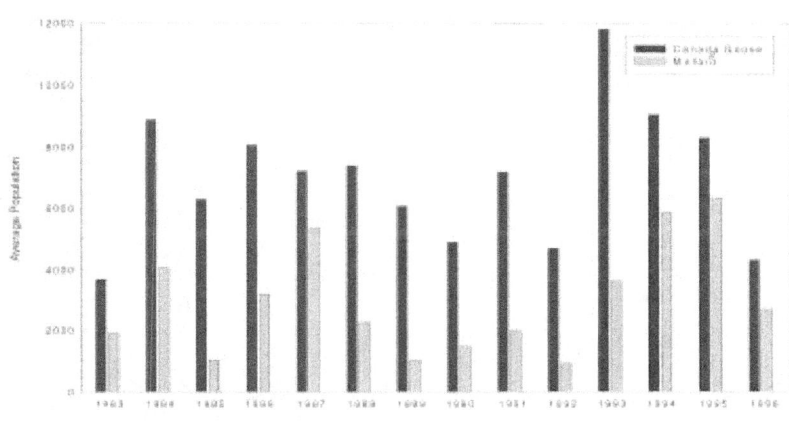

(h)

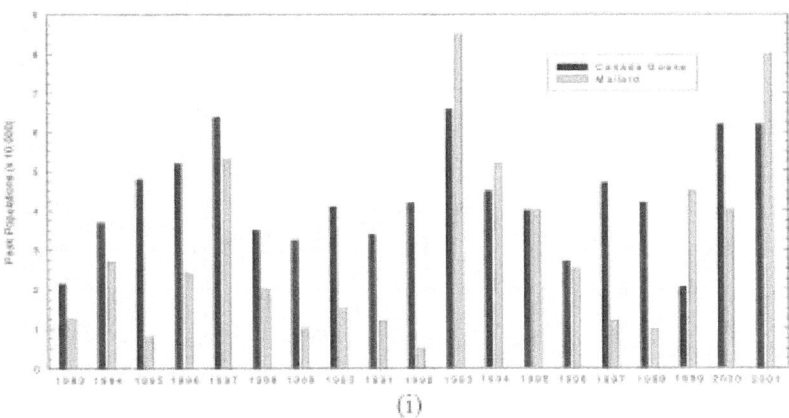

(i)

Appendix D.

Conservation status of avian species known to occur on Kirwin National Wildlife Refuge based on various regional and national plans.

Appendix D. Conservation status of avian species known to occur on Kirwin National Wildlife Refuge based on various regional and national plans. Species listed in Birds of Conservation Concern and the Prairie Avifaunal Biome of the North American Landbird Conservation Plan are denoted with an "X". Designations listed in the Shorebird Plan are as follows: P- = priority species; B, M, W = high concentrations of breeding, migrating, and wintering, respectively; B, M, W = common or locally abundant breeding, migrating, or wintering in region, respectively; b, m, w = uncommon to fairly common breeding, migrating, wintering in region. Population numbers listed under the North American Waterfowl Management Plan represent population objectives for the mid-continent region (K = thousands, M = millions).

Species	Birds of Conservation Concern 2002			American Landbird Conservation Plan		Central Plains and Playa Lakes Region Shorebird Plan	North American Waterbird Conservation Plan Conservation Concern	North American Waterfowl Management Plan
	BCR 19	Region 6	National	Watch	Stewardship			
LOONS								
Common Loon							To Be Assessed	
GREBES								
Horned Grebe							To Be Assessed	
Eared Grebe							Moderate	
Western Grebe							Moderate	
Pied-billed Grebe							To Be Assessed	
PELICANS								
American White Pelican							Moderate	
SWANS/GEESE/DUCKS								
Greater White-fronted Goose								600 K
Snow Goose								1.0 M
Trumpeter Swan								2.5 K
Tundra Swan								80 K
Gadwall								1.5 M
American Wigeon								3.0 M

Species	Birds of Conservation Concern 2002			American Landbird Conservation Plan		Central Plains and Playa Lakes Region Shorebird Plan	North American Waterbird Conservation Plan Conservation Concern	North American Waterfowl Management Plan
	BCR 19	Region 6	National	Watch	Stewardship			
Mallard								8.2 M
Blue-winged Teal								4.7 M
Cinnamon Teal								
Northern Shoveler								2.0 M
Northern Pintail								5.6 M
Green-winged Teal								1.9 M
Canvasback								540 K
Redhead								640 K
Greater Scaup								6.3 M
Lesser Scaup								
GALLINACEOUS BIRDS								
Greater Prairie-Chicken					X			
CORMORANTS								
Double-crested Cormorant							Not At Risk	
HERONS/EGRETS/BITTERNS								
American Bittern							To Be Assessed	
Least Bittern							To Be Assessed	
Great Blue Heron							Not At Risk	
Great Egret							Not At Risk	

Species	Birds of Conservation Concern 2002			American Landbird Conservation Plan		Central Plains and Playa Lakes Region Shorebird Plan	North American Waterbird Conservation Plan Conservation Concern	North American Waterfowl Management Plan
	BCR 19	Region 6	National	Watch	Stewardship			
Snowy Egret							High	
Little Blue Heron	X		X				High	
Cattle Egret							Not At Risk	
Green Heron							Low	
Black-crowned Night-Heron							**Moderate**	
Yellow-crowned Night-Heron							**Moderate**	
White-faced Ibis							**Low**	
HAWKS/KITES/FALCONS/EAGLES								
Mississippi Kite	X				X			
Northern Harrier	X	X	X					
Swainson's Hawk	X	X	X	X				
Ferruginous Hawk		X	X					
Golden Eagle		X						
Peregrine Falcon	X	X	X					
Prairie Falcon		X	X					
RAILS								
Virginia Rail							To Be Assessed	
Sora							To Be Assessed	
American Coot							To Be Assessed	

Species	Birds of Conservation Concern 2002			American Landbird Conservation Plan		Central Plains and Playa Lakes Region Shorebird Plan	North American Waterbird Conservation Plan Conservation Concern	North American Waterfowl Management Plan
	BCR 19	Region 6	National	Watch	Stewardship			
CRANES								
Sandhill Crane							To Be Assessed	
Whooping Crane							To Be Assessed	
SHOREBIRDS								
Black-bellied Plover						M		
American Golden-Plover		X	X			P-M		
Snowy Plover	X	X	X			P-M, B		
Semipalmated Plover						M		
Piping Plover						**P-M, B**		
Killdeer						M, W, B		
Black-necked Stilt						M, b		
American Avocet						**P-M, B**		
Greater Yellowlegs						M		
Lesser Yellowlegs						M		
Willet						M, b		
Spotted Sandpiper						M, w, B		
Upland Sandpiper		X	X			**P-M, B**		
Long-billed Curlew	X	X	X			**P-M, B**		
Hudsonian Godwit	X	X	X			P-M		

Species	Birds of Conservation Concern 2002 BCR 19	Region 6	National	American Landbird Conservation Plan Watch	Stewardship	Central Plains and Playa Lakes Region Shorebird Plan	North American Waterbird Conservation Plan Conservation Concern	North American Waterfowl Management Plan
Marbled Godwit			X			m		
Ruddy Turnstone						m		
Sanderling						m		
Semipalmated Sandpiper						P-M		
Western Sandpiper						M		
Least Sandpiper						P-M, W		
White-rumped Sandpiper						P-M		
Baird's Sandpiper						P-M		
Dunlin						m		
Stilt Sandpiper			X			P-M		
Long-billed Dowitcher						P-M, W		
Common Snipe						M, W, b		
Wilson's Phalarope	X	X	X			M, b		
GULLS								
Franklin's Gull							Moderate	
Bonaparte's Gull							Moderate	
Ring-billed Gull							Not At Risk	
Herring Gull							Low	
Glaucous Gull							Not At Risk	

44

Species	Birds of Conservation Concern 2002			American Landbird Conservation Plan		Central Plains and Playa Lakes Region Shorebird Plan	North American Waterbird Conservation Plan Conservation Concern	North American Waterfowl Management Plan
	BCR 19	Region 6	National	Watch	Stewardship			
TERNS								
Caspian Tern							Low	
Common Tern			X				Low	
Forster's Tern							Moderate	
Least Tern			X				High	
Black Tern							Moderate	
CUCKOOS								
Black-billed Cuckoo		X	X					
Yellow-billed Cuckoo			X					
OWLS								
Burrowing Owl		X	X					
Short-eared Owl		X	X	X				
WOODPECKERS								
Red-headed Woodpecker	X	X	X	X				
FLYCATCHERS								
Willow flycatcher				X				
Scissor-tailed Flycatcher	X		X					
SHRIKES								
Loggerhead Shrike		X	X					

Species	Birds of Conservation Concern 2002			American Landbird Conservation Plan		Central Plains and Playa Lakes Region Shorebird Plan	North American Waterbird Conservation Plan Conservation Concern	North American Waterfowl Management Plan
	BCR 19	Region 6	National	Watch	Stewardship			
VIREOS								
Bell's Vireo	X	X	X	X				
LARKS								
Horned Lark			X					
WARBLERS								
Prairie Warbler			X					
BLACKBIRDS/GROSBEAKS/JUNCOS/SPARROWS								
American Tree Sparrow					X			
Brewer's Sparrow		X	X		X			
Lark Bunting					X			
Grasshopper Sparrow		X	X		X			
Harris's Sparrow	X				X			
Lapland Longspur					X			
Chestnut-collared Longspur	X	X			X			
Dickcissel		X			X			
Bobolink		X